T0356457

world an essential lesson: the importance of nurturing family bonds, cultivating communities through personal connections, and honoring the traditions that bind us together. I am proud that Guardiagrele plays such a pivotal role in this book. I'm confident that readers will find something truly valuable within these pages."

—Flora Bianco, vice mayor of Guardiagrele, Abruzzo, Italy

"In *The Italian Soul*, Judith Valente shows that rich, life-enhancing cultures still exist and that we can tap into their wisdom to strengthen our own. From the centuries-old tradition of chiacchiera, or desultory conversation between strangers leaning against the same sun-struck wall, to the practice of *fare bella figura*—the tradition of looking one's best for the sake of other people— Valente beautifully conveys the intricate web of age-old custom and mutual respect that makes for a fully flourishing society. I love this book."

—Paula Huston, author of *The Hermits of Big Sur*,
Simplifying the Soul, and *A Season of Mystery*

"This gem of a book will make you long to have more 'dolce vita' in your own life"

—Michael N. McGregor, author of *An Island to Myself*,
The Last Grand Tour, and *Pure Act*

THE

Italian
Soul

THE
Italian
Soul

HOW TO SAVOR THE FULL JOYS OF LIFE

JUDITH VALENTE

This edition first published in 2025 by Hampton Roads Publishing,
an imprint of Red Wheel/Weiser, LLC

With offices at:
     65 Parker Street, Suite 7
     Newburyport, MA 01950

Sign up for our newsletter and special offers by going to
     www.redwheelweiser.com/newsletter

Cover image and design by Sky Peck Design
Interior photos by Judith Valente, Leila Caramanico
Interior by Brittany Craig
Typeset in Adobe Jenson Pro

ISBN: 978-1-64297-072-2

Library of Congress Cataloging-in-Publication Data available upon request.

Printed in the United States of America
IBI

10 9 8 7 6 5 4 3 2 1

FSC
MIX
Paper
FSC® C183721

For my grandparents, Benedict and Elvira Costanza and Tommaso and Giovanna Valente, whose courage allowed our family to bridge a life between Italy and the United States; for Dr. Jessica Sciubba and her parents—Pierino Sciubba and Giovanna Di Crescenzo—and my dear cousin Mario Valente, all of whom helped me find my way back to my true home in Italy, and as always, for my beautiful husband Charles Reynard.

Contents

Acknowledgments

Grateful acknowledgment is extended to Dr. Leila Caramanico of Abruzzo, who introduced me to many of the people and places you meet in this book; Franco Malatesta of Cassino for sharing his wisdom and life experience; Carlo Iacovella, for teaching me about the history and culture of Abruzzo; my agent, Amanda Annis of Trident Media Group in New York, for believing in this book and working tirelessly to bring it into the world, as well as Olivia Vella and Aurora Fernandez of Trident Media; Michael Pye and the editorial and marketing staff of Hampton Roads/Red Wheel/Weiser Books as well as former editor Greg Brandenburgh who first introduced me to the Hampton Roads family; and all those quoted in this book either by name or not who helped me to understand the beauty of the Italian soul.

My grandfather, Benedict Costanza, who emigrated from Messina, Sicily, with one of his prize eggplants grown in his garden in New Jersey.

Pursuing the Sweet Life

This is a book about love. My love as an Italian American for the home of my ancestors, a land that Dante called *Il bel paese dove il "Sì" suona.* "The beautiful country where the 'Yes' resounds." It represents the culmination of a quest. A quest to nurture in myself that same propensity for living fully that I find in my Italian friends—an attitude that looks out at the world with a sense of openness, attention, and wonder.

Whenever I am in Italy, my experiences seem more immediate and intense. I am by nature a hard-charging American, often afflicted with a dual diagnosis of workaholism and over-achieverism, always trying to fit more into my days and seemingly never having enough time. In Italy, I somehow have time enough for everything—work, play, family, friends, cooking, cleaning, walking, exercising, and, yes, simply doing nothing. Whenever I leave, it is with the haunting intimation that I can indeed reinvent my life in the States to be just as balanced and enchanting.

I depart Italy always with the same feeling: I found what I was looking for. I have experienced that feeling in only one other context—on visits to monastic communities. Because I write books that aim to help busy people like myself slow down and live more reflective lives, I've spent considerable time in monasteries—studying, praying, and seeking to learn from men and women who want to rise beyond the superficialities of daily life, who yearn to see what Saint Bernard of Clairvaux called *the real behind the real.* In short, who seek a more contemplative life.

What do I mean by a "contemplative life"? It is an attitude of the heart that allows us to see in the simple, mundane elements of daily living both the sacred and the poetic. It is a prescription for experiencing meaning and joy. Repeatedly, I witness that attitude in my Italian friends. It seems to come naturally to them, something passed on through the genes from one generation to the next.

This book is an attempt to distill those contemplative aspects of Italian life that we can absorb into our hard-driving American culture. What you will find in these pages are not complicated self-help prescriptions. Rather, these are love notes, dispatches from my many extended stays across Italy in both major cities and small towns—first as a student, later as a journalist, and most recently as a humble appreciator and observer of daily Italian life.

I write for lovers of Italy who have visited the country often and who will be able to compare notes from their experiences with mine. I write also for those considering a first visit, and for students of the Italian language and culture. I write especially for those seeking to deepen their interior life and follow a spiritual path that travels beyond institutional religion, but does not necessarily dismiss it. A path that does not depend solely on a particular doctrine, but recognizes that the sacred also abides in the simple practices and activities of daily life. Picture yourself walking beside me through narrow streets, peering through half-open windows, catching snippets of conversation and glimpses of the practices, customs, and traditions of a people who look upon living as an art.

There is much to admire about Italy: its remarkable history, storied art and architecture, superb food, classic wines, and elevated aesthetic sense, be it in fashion or product design. What I appreciate most is its gentler, more balanced way of life—what might be described in a kind of shorthand as *la dolce vita*, the sweet life. My Italian friends taught me to value the sanctity of the dinner table. I learned from them to prize quality over quantity, to recognize when enough is enough. They introduced me to the simple practice of building community through *chiacchiera*, the tradition of ad hoc chitchat that goes on daily in cafés and grocery shops, on street corners, park benches, and even in doctors' offices (a favored meeting place for sharing news and opinions). Italy taught me to pay attention to self-care as diligently as I care for my career. To pride myself on relationships as much as professional achievements.

I learned an important lesson about balancing priorities when a friend, who lives in the town of San Vito Chietino on the Adriatic coast, asked me to lunch one Sunday at her home. She invited her parents as well. Throughout Italy, the Sunday meal with family remains a sacrosanct tradition. I usually publish a column on Sundays on Medium.com and hadn't finished writing it yet. I brought my laptop computer to the lunch, figuring I could finish my writing before the meal began. When I started typing at the coffee table, my friend's mother looked at me quizzically. I explained to her that I needed to complete some work.

"It's Sunday!" she exclaimed.

I shut down the computer and kept it out of view for the rest of the afternoon.

The heart of the lesson came later that day. When lunch was over, we all went for a long, leisurely walk along the Adriatic seashore. I remember the walk vividly because I was so touched by how my thirty-six-year-old friend still strolled arm and arm with her parents, and how the sea air refreshed all of us after our delightful, multicourse meal. I finished writing my column later in the day, in plenty of time to publish it. I didn't have to sacrifice time in the company of friends. I could enjoy a delicious meal, relax, take a stroll, and still get my work done. For all that, I have my friend's wise Italian mother to thank.

One of my coauthors over the years has been Brother Paul Quenon, a Trappist monk of the famous Abbey of Gethsemani in Kentucky, where the great spirituality author Thomas Merton once lived. When I left my full-time job in broadcast journalism to focus on writing books, I lamented to Brother Paul that I couldn't seem to arrive at a proper working rhythm. I felt I was flailing around, wasting too much of my day. He wrote back: "Indeed, a good way of getting over the feeling that you are wasting your time is to go out and waste more of it. Waste it intentionally. Take a walk in the neighborhood and see the trees; notice how people keep their yards. Smell the air. Get free of what seems urgent and necessary; get away from the feeling that the world will crumble without you."

Brother Paul described a "free gift" he said he had received the previous evening. It was the sight of a full moon pouring a gauzy, mother-of-pearl white over the fields surrounding his abbey. "To see a sight like this is rare," he wrote. "You must be there." My friend's Italian mother would wholeheartedly agree. Such pauses are moments of grace, what Italians might call *il dolce far niente*, the sweet do-nothing. They are also pathways to experiencing the sacred. They allow us to experience the blessings of life and creation through small cracks of wonder in our daily existence.

Italy also gave me a greater appreciation of a word that is integral to the monastic, contemplative life, but that we hear all too infrequently these days in our American public discourse. That word is *community*. As our world sinks more deeply into a pool of Me-ism—of them against us—our sense of the common good is in jeopardy of drowning as well. That became clear when so much rage erupted during the Covid-19 pandemic over vaccine and mask mandates. I traveled to Italy in 2021 just as the omicron variant had begun to surge. I took a shuttle bus to Chicago's O'Hare International Airport at a time when face masks were still mandated on public transportation. The gentleman seated behind me had his mask pulled down under his chin. I waited to see if he eventually would pull it up and cover his face. When he didn't, I politely reminded him of the announcement the driver had made about wearing our masks. He reacted by launching a stream of expletives at me. It caused such a ruckus that the driver threatened to stop the bus if this passenger didn't calm down.

When I arrived in the small Italian town where I was to stay for three months, I noticed how everyone I saw adhered to the national mandate for masks in both indoor and outdoor public places. In churches, large green dots pasted onto the pews ensured socially distanced seating. Bottles of hand sanitizer were placed near the entrance. At communion time, before receiving the host in their hands, people would fish into their pockets or purses and pop open personal-sized bottles of sanitizer, then look around to offer their bottles to others. It was a small gesture of kindness, but a measure too of fostering community, of saying we are all in this together.

That same spirit was on broad display in other ways. Italy was one of the first countries struck by the coronavirus pandemic, and among the hardest hit. Italians didn't show up at government buildings brandishing guns to protest stay-at-home orders and school and business closings, as some Americans did. Quarantined in narrow houses and cramped apartments, neighbors instead serenaded one another from their balconies, singing and playing musical instruments. To shore up everyone's spirits, nurses broadcast the Italian national anthem over loudspeakers in hospital wards. Italians showed the rest of the world how to meet trauma and tragedy with beauty and grace.

The strong interior pull I feel for Italy originated with my four grandparents. As the youngest grandchild, I did not know much about three of those grandparents. My paternal grandfather, Tommaso Valente, died before I was born. My mother's mother, Elvira Tedeschi Costanza, passed away when I was four.

My father's mother, Giovanna Mastronardi Valente, endured frequent hospitalizations, which meant I had few encounters with her before she died when I was thirteen. That grandmother became a cipher I puzzled over throughout my life. Interestingly, she became the ancestor most responsible for my rediscovering my Italian roots.

When I began studying monastic spirituality, I visited the famous Abbey of Monte Cassino about ninety miles south of Rome. Saint Benedict, the founder of Western monasticism, lived his final years at Monte Cassino and it is where he wrote his famous *Rule* for monastic life. Monks and monastic sisters still follow that fifteen-hundred-year-old text today, as do an increasing number of laypeople like me, who seek to live the monastic values of community, consensus, hospitality, prayer, and praise in daily, secular life. Only afterward, in conversations with my older cousins, did I learn that my grandmother Giovanna had grown up in Cassino. She would have seen the Abbey of Monte Cassino every day of her life before emigrating to America, as the monastery dominates the city from its mountaintop perch. Suddenly the genesis of my fascination with monastic life became clear. It was as though I had been hardwired by my genes to develop a passion for contemplative living. My Italian heritage led me there.

The one grandparent I did know well was my maternal grandfather, Benedict Costanza. He lived to the age of ninety-five and spent part of each year with my aunt and uncle who lived on the second floor of my parents' two-family home in Bayonne, New Jersey. Grandpa Costanza told me of his early life in the Sicilian seaside city of Messina and of his ocean voyage to America, which sounded to my five-year-old imagination like an adventure movie plot. He eventually sponsored his parents and all six of his siblings to come to America. The drawback for me was that virtually none of that side of the family remained in Italy. Nor did my grandfather or any of his siblings ever return to their native land. Still, our Italian roots never faded from view. They remained like an invisible magnet, connecting us to something beyond our middle-class American life.

I still have the black-and-white, marble-covered composition book in which my grandfather jotted down in his old-world-style handwriting Italian words for me to memorize: *La madre. Il padre. La sorella. Il fratello.* When he told of licking the salt from his skin after swimming as a boy in the waters off the coast of Messina, I could taste the sea salt as well. I finally had the chance to visit Italy for the first time on a class trip as a junior in high school. I felt more at home there than in the country where I had been born. From my grandparents, I carry within me the seed of a dual-layered identity. To this day, their example helps me combine the best of my Italian heritage with what I cherish in American culture. They gave me the gift of living with two cultures interwoven in a single soul.

There is a lovely Italian idiom, *all'Italiana*. It derives from the expression, *alla maniera italiana*: in the Italian manner. It is more than a style, though. It connotes a way of life. I hope these pages will help you to bridge our American culture with the attitudes, traditions, and practices that make Italian life a model for experiencing a sense of the sacred amid the many demands and distractions of ordinary living. Though this is not a travel book, it is a place for readers to travel along. Within these pages, it is possible to come and go, read and rest. Think of it as a platter, offering several diverse spiritual "recipes" for nourishing the soul.

The Irish poet and theologian John O'Donohue has written, "Always in a pilgrimage there is a change of mind and a change of heart." May the time you spend as a pilgrim within these pages touch your heart in ways that bring a taste of the Italian *dolce vita* into your own home. I invite you to sit in your favorite reading chair and let your soul travel vicariously with me. *Buon viaggio!*

CHAPTER 1

The Art of Conversation

My friend Pierino wakes early. He bids his wife Giovanna goodbye and heads to Piazza Santa Maria Maggiore in the center of his hometown of Guardiagrele in the Abruzzo region of Italy. There, he meets men he has known since childhood. They stand at the counter of one of the nearby cafés with one foot resting on a brass rail while they sip an *espresso* or *caffè macchiato.* Then they congregate for a few hours under the 14th-century stone archways surrounding the piazza. Talking.

One of the first things you notice when you spend any amount of time in Italy is the amount of talking that goes on. There is even a specific word for it: *chiacchiera.* It describes a kind of desultory, stream-of-consciousness chitchat often meant to

Men engaged in the important art of conversation or *chiacchiera*.

simply pass the time. It might take place milling about a piazza, sitting on a park bench, standing in front of a church, or even in the waiting room of a doctor's office. These are not the kind of quick exchanges that take place over a cell phone. They are tête-à-tête conversations that spill out from sidewalk cafés and the insides of bars, from hidden courtyards and the open windows of families sharing a meal at home.

For centuries, Italians have shown how gifted they are in art, architecture, cuisine, fashion, and design. They have made an art of conversation as well. In an age of increased cocooning, where one needn't get out of bed to purchase groceries, watch a film, or play a game of cards, Italians still prefer to be out and about. They like to see and be seen. There are no particular protocols in *chiacchiera* for what gets discussed. The men who meet in the Piazza Santa Maria Maggiore might expound one day on the condition of local roads and sidewalks, and the next share news of a family member who emigrated to the United States. They might argue over their favorite soccer team's latest loss or dissect the most recent twist in Italy's serpentine national politics.

Mother Teresa once famously observed that "the great American illness" isn't heart disease or cancer. It is loneliness. For Italians, getting outside and engaging in conversation ward off isolation. It just might be a cause of their longevity as well. Though the Covid pandemic lowered the life expectancy of

Italians to 82 years from 83, theirs still exceeds that of Americans by four years. Italy continues to have one of the oldest populations in all of Europe. Meanwhile, the longevity of Americans is declining in contrast to that of other advanced countries. High rates of suicide, alcoholism, and drug addiction in the United States are partly to blame. Not surprisingly, those problems often grow out of a sense of loneliness, self-isolation, and lack of belonging.

While such problems certainly exist in Italy, they aren't nearly as prevalent. Access to universal health care and a tradition of eating fresh, locally grown, and high-quality food also play a role in insuring Italians enjoy a long life. Still, I can't help but think that experiencing a sense of community—feeling that you matter and that you belong—is also what infuses older Italians with the wherewithal to soldier on.

Franco Malatesta is a remarkably spry widower in his eighties. Franco lives in my paternal grandmother's birthplace of Cassino, about a ninety-minute drive from Rome. Each afternoon he climbs three flights of stairs to his apartment, carrying a sack of groceries in each hand, and cooks up a plate of pasta and vegetables. Every morning, he strolls to the Caffè Palace, about a fifteen-minute walk from his apartment, to be with his buddies. Another facet of Italian life: People don't just talk a lot, they also walk.

Franco's friends jokingly refer to the Caffè Palace as their "office." They are all similar in age, and, like him, retired. Though they haven't reported to an office job for decades, they come to their morning chat-fests dressed in crisply ironed shirts, often complemented by a sweater or vest. Franco usually can be spotted from blocks away by his trademark black fedora and camel-colored leather jacket.

The men discuss the news in the morning paper, lament the inability of their single professional daughters to find suitable husbands, and grouse about their married offspring who haven't yet given them grandchildren. Franco says he misses his wife who has been dead more than twenty years. He quickly adds, though, that he still wakes up looking forward to each day because he knows that every morning his friends at the Palace will be waiting for him.

Cafés aren't the only gathering spots. Waiting rooms in doctors' offices are usually sober places where folks generally seek to avoid even eye contact. One might sit there checking texts or reading a magazine. It's rarely a place to strike up a conversation. Not so Italian doctors' offices. On a recent stay, my husband contracted a bad case of bronchitis and had to go every day for a week to a doctor's office to receive an antibiotic injection. (In large parts of Italy, injections are still given in lieu of pills.) I noticed that some of the same people showed up in the doctor's waiting room day after day. Eventually, I realized they weren't all there for checkups. They come for the chitchat. Like cafés, parks, and piazzas, doctors' offices are a common meeting place to engage with neighbors and friends. (An interesting sidenote: Even as a non-Italian citizen, my husband paid nothing for these health visits, thanks to Italy's national health care).

My Italian teacher, Dr. Jessica Sciubba, once told me about a photograph she cherishes. It is of her grandmother Filomena sitting on a bench with her two best friends, Lina and Maria. "For as long as I can remember and until each of them passed away, those three women spent their afternoons on that bench by the front door of the two-story building where all three lived," my teacher recalled. "Whoever passed by had to stop and chat with them. It was mandatory. Even if a person was in a hurry, just smiling and greeting politely would not have sufficed. My grandmother and her two friends were the guardians of the gateway, the keepers of the fort with its families, stories, and secrets."

The women's conversation might bounce from spiritual matters to superstitions as they sat, knitting and crocheting as they chatted. "Who knows how many blankets and doilies they created in this manner over the years!" my teacher says. "When I think about their friendship, I wish I could find someone I could share a bench with every day, every season, year after year, right outside my doorstep."

This form of bonding isn't limited to the older generation. On a Saturday night in Cassino, where my distant cousin Mario Valente lives, one can barely move through the piazza in front of Sant'Antonio di Padova Church because of the crowd of teenagers gathered there. Doing what? Talking.

On Sunday evenings, families stroll along Cassino's Via San Nicola or Corso della Repubblica. It's an occasion to window-shop, certainly. Mostly, though, it's a time to people-watch, catch up with relatives and friends, and perhaps, just as importantly, to be seen. Saint Benedict, the patron saint of Europe whose monastery watches over Cassino from a mountaintop, started out living as a hermit in a cave. He eventually concluded that being part of a community offered a saner, healthier way to live and began founding monastic communities. It is probably one of the reasons monks and religious sisters residing in community live to a ripe old age, as many Italians do.

To be sure, Italians are being challenged to expand their idea of community. Italy faces a rapid influx of refugees from North Africa who are of a different race and culture and often a different religion. The presence of new arrivals can generate fear, especially when stoked by self-serving "Italy First" or "America First" anti-immigration politicians. One hopes, though, that the gregarious and hospitable Italian spirit so often on display in the cafés, piazzas, parks, and doctors' offices will prove stronger than fear or suspicion in the end. With the newcomers as well as the native-born, may the *chiacchiera* go on. May the art of conversation strengthen the bonds of belonging.

FOR REFLECTION

Do you have a special place to meet with friends and simply chat? What is that experience like?

What are some effective ways you have cultivated for coping with loneliness and building a community of friends and support?

What are some ways in which you can forge a better sense of community where you live?

CHAPTER 2

Fare Bella Figura

When I worked as a reporter for the *Wall Street Journal*, I took a month's leave of absence one year to study Italian at the Dante Alighieri School of Languages in the Tuscan city of Siena. I rented a room in an apartment on Via Quinto Settano, owned by Signora Cristina Livani. *La signora* was a relatively young widow, somewhere between early to mid-fifties. Her contract with the language school required her to prepare two meals a day for me, usually *prima colazione* (breakfast) and *pranzo* (lunch). She was an excellent cook and during our lunches together, she held forth on her two favorite topics: *il cibo e l'amore*, food and love.

Surprisingly, I never saw her go on a date. The fact that her thirty-something son still lived with her well might have damp-ened her love life. What I remember most about Signora Livani is that she never left the house without putting on lipstick, rouge, a silk scarf, a nice blouse and skirt, and high heels, even if it was just to buy biscotti at the neighborhood *panetteria* or pick up a few household items at the Upim department store. Her fastidiousness about her appearance fascinated me. I grew up in a blue-collar neighborhood where women my mother's age would often run to the supermarket wearing a kerchief wrapped around pink hair curlers.

Signora Livani was what you could call a practitioner of *fare bella figura*, the art of making a good impression. She aimed to present the best, most pleasing version or "figure" of herself to the world. She is the reason that to this day I put on makeup to go grocery shopping or attend my Zumba fitness classes, even though the classes are online! I suppose it is part of the same syndrome that makes some of us wash and style our hair before going to the hairdresser.

Of course, in Italy as elsewhere, women generally are held to a higher standard when it comes to appearance. That's not to say Italian men don't also *fare bella figura*. I've spent many pleasant moments observing the fashion aesthetics of Italian men on their way to and from their offices. Their suits rarely sag. Their ties are knotted neither too tightly nor too loosely. Even their sensible rubber-soled shoes have a look of elegance. As one young American exchange student in Florence told me, "My Italian friends dress for school the way I do on my best nights going out on a date."

Likewise, I can usually pick out Americans amid a crowd of Italians even before I hear them speak. I spot them by the fit of their clothes, their style of shoes, and the general casualness of their appearance. I've often wondered what motivates this nonchalance about appearance. Similarly, what's behind my Italian friends' preoccupation with the image they present to the world?

Perhaps part of the answer lies in our American obsession with personal freedom. Clothing is an extension of our individuality. If others don't like how we look, too bad for them. The US is also very much an indoors culture. We drive to the places where we need to go. Our car becomes an extension of home, and of course we dress as we please when we are in our own homes. Italy, by contrast, is a largely outdoor culture. City dwellers who live in cramped apartments need outdoor spaces to *cambiare l'aria*, as they say, to change the air. Piazzas, parks, and other public spaces take on the role of outdoor living rooms. People walk to school, to work, to stores. Walking is a time to be seen. So why not try to look your best?

Presenting a *bella figura* doesn't require spending profligately on one's wardrobe. It might mean buying fewer, but higher-quality clothing and shoes that won't wear out quickly. It entails learning to refresh or dress up the same suit, dress, or blouse with the addition of a scarf, a different purse, a different pair of shoes, or a different tie. It's a form of consumerism that doesn't lend itself to waste—to mountains of clothes and columns of shoes we don't wear and don't need.

Seeking to look one's best and not like an unmade bed has a deeper meaning that goes beyond merely presenting an appealing appearance. It has to do with self-care and respect for oneself and for others. An American woman who married an Italian said she quickly learned to *fare bella figura* early in the marriage when her husband looked at her askance as she tried to dash out to the butcher shop one day wearing a worn-out running suit. "Are you going out in *that?*" the husband asked. "I'm not expecting to run into anyone I know," his wife replied. "Maybe," her husband said, "but the butcher will see you."

Another of my friends recalls being in kindergarten and memorizing a poem she wanted to recite for her mother on Mother's Day. She chose one written in the Abruzzo dialect by Modesto Della Porta, one of that region's most famous poets. With the help of her grandmother, she practiced pronouncing the unfamiliar words. When Mother's Day arrived, my friend wore her favorite dress and waited for the right moment after the family's Sunday lunch ended to stand on a chair and recite the poem.

"I was driven to do my finest by my unconditional love, admiration, and respect for my mother," my friend told me. "*Fare bella figura* is, in the end, really about love. It is about loving others enough to want to look and be your best, and about loving yourself enough to feel good in your skin about what you do."

This isn't merely about manufacturing a façade. It is more like finishing a self-portrait. It is a way of saying I care enough about myself to want to look my best with whatever material God or nature provided. Our Buddhist friends might consider the body an illusion—mere matter that will eventually perish. Still, it is the matter we are given by our Creator. If we care for our bodies, then how can we not also care for our spirit, the deepest part of our self? When we aim for beauty in any form, we offer a gift to the world. As my Italian friends would say, why not paint a beautiful self-portrait?

FOR REFLECTION

Is how you present yourself to others important to you? If not, why not?

What is the impression—the *figura*—you would like to project? How does it reflect your inner spirit, your true self?

If *fare bella figura* is as much about behavior and attitude as it is about appearance, how might its practice change the way you dress, the purchases you make, the way you interact with others?

Fruit stands like this one in Sulmona are ubiquitous.

CHAPTER 3

Poco, Ma Buono

Americans love a bargain. We also love cheap. That's why dollar stores are as ubiquitous in urban shopping districts as on rural roads. Dollar General, Dollar Tree, and the like were among the few retail outlets that didn't suffer during the economic crisis brought on by the Covid-19 pandemic. On the contrary, they thrived. Consumer reports might warn against buying certain bargain-store products—from cereal, milk, and fresh meat to makeup, batteries, and electronic devices. Still, it doesn't seem to put a dent in the great American lust for low prices.

We tend to exalt quantity over quality. In Italy, quality matters. There is even an expression, *poco, ma buono*—little, but good.

I have spent many pleasant visits with my distant cousin Mario, who lives south of Rome in my grandmother's hometown of Cassino. For his signature dish of *linguine alle vongole*—pasta with clam sauce—he could purchase a perfectly serviceable five-hundred-gram package of pasta at the Conad supermarket chain for slightly more than one euro (about $1.10). Instead, he seeks out small shops that sell linguine made through a slow process known as *trafilata al bronzo* (extrusion through bronze dies). It involves a tradition of using bronze instruments instead of steel to shape the pasta. This process gives the pasta a rougher texture, allowing more of the sauce to stick to it. *Trafilata al bronzo* pasta also happens to cost as much as five times more than ordinary linguine. So what do you do? Buy less of the pasta and enjoy the taste more. A case of *meno, ma meglio*—less, but better. Or, as we might say in English, less is more.

Though quality remains a prime consideration for Italian shoppers, the Euro store—the Italian version of Dollar General and Dollar Tree outlets—is becoming a more familiar part of the shopping landscape. Euro stores appear up and down the Italian peninsula, from Trentino to Lazio, Molise to Sicily. Increasingly, too, large supermarket chains like Crai, Conad, and Coop (pronounced by Italians as "coh-up") are attracting growing numbers of patrons by offering lower prices than those found in small, family-run groceries. The chain supermarkets sell perfectly acceptable pasta. It just won't do for many like my cousin Mario who wouldn't consider serving guests one of his signature dishes using a mass-produced chain brand.

An Italian friend who moved to the US tells me she soon learned to practice *poco, ma buono* shopping for food in the States as well. "I immediately realized that in order to keep eating in the manner to which I was accustomed—with fresh ingredients and products imported from Italy—it would require a far bigger budget than my salary afforded," she said. "I did not want to completely alter my eating habits by ingesting processed food or purchasing low-quality pasta or produce. So, *poco, ma buono* became a way of life. I adapted my diet to whatever fresh produce the local markets had to offer on sale, and spruced it up with some carefully chosen, good-quality ingredients . . . even if that meant buying lesser quantities."

The principle of *poco, ma buono* applies to more than food. I once shopped for a leather purse in the Abruzzo town of Orsogna, which has a large weekday street market. I was drawn immediately to a medium-sized brown and white handbag that resembled a designer purse and contained smaller-size purses within it for storing makeup, a cell phone, and eyeglasses. It had arm straps and also came with a longer strap you could attach to turn the purse into a shoulder bag. The price was good too: 20 euros. Just the amount I was willing to spend.

When an old Italian street vender saw my selection, he shook his finger over the handbag. He directed me to a smaller cream-colored purse. *Fatto in Italia*, he said, as if imparting a major secret. "Made in Italy." The purse that had initially caught my eye most assuredly was mass-produced in China and made of synthetic material. The *fatto in Italia* purse, he explained, was genuine leather. It also cost 20 euros more than the other one. In my bargain-hunting mode, I wondered if the vendor was simply looking to make a better sale. I ended up buying the cheaper, synthetic purse—because it came with more bells and whistles, for less money.

Later, an Italian friend told me that she also had purchased the same style handbag. After a year of use, its strap broke. The straps to my own purse soon began showing wear as did the bottom of the purse, so much so that I worried it might end up with a hole and the contents might one day all come tumbling out when I was walking down a street. I had not yet learned the lesson of *poco, ma buono*.

My adventure in purse-shopping ultimately has a happy ending. On a subsequent visit, I again searched for a handbag. This time, I settled on a leather purse made by the Italian manufacturer Carpisa. It is creamy white, smooth to the touch, and lovely to look at, right down to the perfectly straight stitching along its sides and straps. It is probably one of the nicest items in my wardrobe: "classic and timeless," as Carpisa says of its handbags. I bought it with the help of an Italian friend in a department store during a January post-Christmas sale. It cost quite a bit more than the purse I had purchased in the outdoor market in Orsogna. I expect, though, that my new purse, Italian-made of genuine leather, will last for quite a long time. If I take good care of it, I might never have to buy another purse to replace it. Saved by the beauty of *poco, ma buono*!

When I first began visiting monasteries, one of the Benedictine sisters I met gave me this handy expression for avoiding the lure of unnecessary purchases: Do I really need this, and do I need it *now*? It's a prescription for avoiding the kind of impulsive purchases that clutter our homes and eventually clog our landfills when we finally throw out what we no longer want and probably didn't need in the first place. In that sense, *poco, ma buono* offers a spiritual lesson as well. It is a way of caring for creation. We release the urge to acquire more and still more things that can detract us from what is truly important. It allows us to focus on what we truly need. It is a way of saying we value quality more than quantity. It is a way of recognizing when enough is enough.

FOR REFLECTION

How would you describe your purchasing practices?

Are your buying habits in line with your spiritual values? In what ways?

Does *poco, ma buono*—placing quality over quantity—make sense to you? How might it change what and how you buy?

Life-size statues of saints, like this one with real hair of the Madonna del Carmine in Abruzzo, lend a certain earthiness to depictions of the saints.

CHAPTER 4

A Bloody Jesus, a Madonna with Real Hair

The Catholic Church, if not quite dead yet, is certainly comatose in several European countries. Italy, though, is an exception. To be sure, only about half the population regularly attends Sunday Mass, and most of those churchgoers are women. Financial scandals within the Vatican, the clergy sex abuse crisis, as well as the institutional church's opposition to divorce, abortion, and same-sex marriage, have driven away many—especially the young. Still, there can be no doubt that this is a Catholic country. It isn't so much a matter of Italians fervently embracing the teachings of the Church. They don't. Both divorce and abortion became legal in Italy in the 1970s over the Vatican's objections. Rather, Italy's idiosyncratic brand of Catholicism remains alive even among the nonpracticing because it is enmeshed in the culture, in everyday sights, in national traditions.

I credit this, in part, to the ubiquitous presence of churches. A common joke is that even though food is of the utmost importance to Italian culture, there are still more churches in Italy than grocery stores. You have to walk only a few blocks in any direction to find a church. Usually these are ready-made oases of peace and quiet in the midst of bustling cities. Italian churches are often cooler than the outside in the summer and warmer in winter. Church doors remain open at all hours, infusing every neighborhood with a constant reminder of the sacred. Walking into US churches built after the 1950s often feels like entering an amphitheater or, worse, a barn. It seems as though modern American architects decided with Puritan fervor to dispense with the statues, frescoes, marble pillars, and vaulted ceilings that make entering centuries-old Italian churches such an ethereal experience.

One of the main characteristics of Italian churches is their expressive, life-size statues. My paternal grandparents were married in the Church of Sant'Antonio di Padova, a splendid example of Romanesque architecture in the city of Cassino. Just to the left as you enter is a large plaster statue of Jesus lying in his tomb. This is not a serene, otherworldly Jesus. Red paint made to look hauntingly like real blood drips from this Jesus's hands, feet, and side. The expression on his face is that of a man experiencing excruciating pain. Gazing on this all-too-human-looking Jesus, you can't help but imagine in your own body his immense agony during the crucifixion.

Representations of the Virgin Mary are equally striking. On a side aisle of Sant'Antonio, a wooden statue of Mary stands with a crown of stars above her head. The stars actually light up. They seem to do so on their own without any obvious power source, inviting those who gaze at the statue to imagine that some kind of divine force is causing the light.

My favorite figure of the Virgin, though, is the life-size version of *La Madonna del Carmine*, Our Lady of Mount Carmel, that stares out from a glass case above the altar of a little church in an out-of-the-way piazza in the Abruzzo town of Guardiagrele. She is dressed in a maroon and gold embroidered gown, like something out of a Renaissance ball. The thing I just love about her is that she has real hair—flowing, straight, shoulder-length chestnut hair. Not everyone is so impressed, though. My friend Giovanna Di Crescenzo from Guardiagrele tells me that when her daughter was small she was so frightened by the statue's real hair that the little girl would cry every time they went inside the church.

When I experienced a health challenge in my own life, I asked my friend Giovanna to email me a photo of *La Madonna del Carmine*. She snapped the picture on her phone from such an angle that if I zoomed in on it, I could feel as though I were actually sitting in one of the pews, looking straight up at the statue. I spent time each day gazing at *La Madonna*. As it turned out, my condition was actually far less serious than the original diagnosis suggested. Was it the time I spent with *La Madonna del Carmine* that made a difference? Who can say? It is comforting to me, at any rate, to attribute that change in fortune to my dark-haired friend staring down from her altar perch. I will always be grateful to her.

There is another life-size statue of the Madonna across town in Guardiagrele's Church of San Francesco. There, a blonde version of the Virgin stands with her feet crushing an animal so monstrous-looking that it would haunt any child's nighttime dreams. In a room behind the altar lie the remains of San Nicola Greco. A replica of his shriveled head and emaciated corpse dressed in a monk's black habit reclines in a glass case. Such macabre sights are not unusual in Italian churches. The dismembered, mummified head of Saint Catherine of Siena is encased in that city's Basilica of San Domenico, along with her right thumb. People travel from across the world to see Saint Catherine's body parts. Thousands also make pilgrimages to the city of Cascia, in the region of Umbria, to pray before the withered foot of Santa Rita of Cascia. Santa Rita suffered so much physical and emotional pain in her life that she is the saint to whom Italians (and now I too) pray in seemingly hopeless situations.

One reason the church survives is that its customs and rituals are entwined with public holidays and celebrations. The Feast of the Epiphany on January 6 is a work holiday throughout the country. So is the Catholic holy day of the Assumption of Mary on August 15, known also as *Ferragosto*, a blending of the words *feria* for holiday and *Agosto* for August. The Assumption, however, is a holy day most Italians celebrate, not by going to church, but by going to the beach or to the mountains. Good Friday is another national holiday, as is the Monday after Easter, when it is traditional to go picnicking.

Good Friday provides the opportunity for one of Italy's largest communal events, as both large and small communities participate in a traditional *Via Crucis*, or Way of the Cross, procession. The spectacle usually begins in the town's central piazza with a statue of the Madonna dressed in a long black mourning dress and lace mantilla being carried on a platform, followed by a statue of Christ, crucified, lying in a glass coffin. A priest intones the Stations of the Cross and a chorus of men in black monk-style cowls sing hymns in Latin while residents from the town parade behind them.

Almost every town has its patron saint, and celebrations honoring those patrons are also an important part of the cultural glue that binds Italians to their Catholic roots. For many young Italians who have cut ties with the institutional church, these celebrations still evoke a distinct nostalgia, if not actual reverence. A friend of mine in her thirties explains that, like many in her millennial generation, she long ago stopped subscribing to the dogma of the Catholic Church. Still, she says, "These celebrations are part of my communal sense of identity and belonging."

Each year on August 7, my friend attends the celebration of her hometown of Guardiagrele's patron saint, San Donato. No one I asked in the town could tell me why San Donato is their patron. There is no record of him ever visiting Guardiagrele. What's more, about sixty other Italian towns claim San Donato as their patron, too. He is believed to have worked miracles for those suffering convulsions, and that has been enough to cement his peripatetic reputation since the Middle Ages.

The San Donato pageant is quite the spectacle and unfolds each year in the same way. It starts with a marching band, followed by a procession of women dressed in multicolored embroidered dresses who parade through the streets, balancing copper vases filled with flowers on their heads. A priest follows in a flowing white sacramental robe along with an altar boy carrying a metal cross. Next comes the life-size statue of San Donato, carried on a sort of throne by a group of hardy men. At the sight of the statue, those watching on the sidelines bend their knees and make the sign of the cross. They, too, then join in the procession, dressed for the occasion in their summer finery.

My thirty-something friend says she likes to remain on the sidelines, so as not to be mistaken for having a religious interest in the proceedings. "Though I do not join in, I follow my own ritual within the ritual—that of being an observer on the margins. And that keeps me connected to the community in my own way," she says.

I once drove an Italian visitor around Washington, DC, on one of her first visits to the US. She was astonished by the multiplicity of Christian denominations she saw, often within blocks of a synagogue or a mosque. "There are too many religions in this country!" she proclaimed. For me, this ability to accommodate religious diversity without tearing the fabric of society is a credit to the US and a source of its cultural strength. Still, I love the many communal experiences of faith one encounters in Italy, and yearn sometimes for more of those shared religious expressions where I live. In Italy, those expressions might take the form of a statue of the Virgin peering out from an alcove in a private home, or a religious mural painted on the side of a public building, or else, as in the case of the *Via Crucis* and San Donato festivals, a colorful community procession.

Though these traditions emerge from Catholicism, one doesn't need to be a card-carrying Catholic to sense the transcendent unfolding in them. At a basic level, these rituals can help us feel more deeply connected to the contemplative aspects of daily life, whatever faith tradition we follow. While much of religious expression is an individual, personal matter, Italy shows that there are ways to cultivate a communal appreciation of the Divine. Through them, it is possible to experience a kind of soul-soothing expression that unites us with others, whether one is overtly religious or not. It doesn't require embarking on an individual quest to find the sacred. It is a collective journey that we can share and enjoy with the community around us.

FOR REFLECTION

What types of religious rituals or imagery are you drawn to?

What churches have left an indelible impression on you and what was it about them that impressed you?

Have you ever watched or been in a public religious procession, such as a *Via Crucis*? What was the experience like?

CHAPTER 5

That All Might Be Remembered

When my mother died suddenly of a stroke in 2001, the wake, funeral Mass, and burial took place over two days. I remember the moment my siblings and I watched my mother's coffin lowered into the ground. It felt as though we had arrived at a significant endpoint in our grieving process and had permission now to return to "normal" life.

For Italians, the burial of a loved one isn't an end. It's the beginning of a new kind of relationship. *Nonno, Nonna, Papà,* or *Mamma* aren't gone. They are still part of the family, still present, but now in a different way. This is perhaps why Italian graveyards are more like extensions of the home than the spare, silent, joyless places many US cemeteries can be.

Because of the threat of earthquakes, Italians usually bury their dead aboveground in marble and stone crypts. As one of my friends explained, "It is better than sticking your loved one in the dirt." Crypts often contain ceramic images or laminated photographs of the deceased. Seeing an image of the person makes him or her seem far more real than a name etched on a tombstone. Gravesites are as well-tended as any backyard or public garden. Families plant flowers and trees nearby or else leave flowers in metal vases. I once spotted a three-foot-high, fully decorated Christmas tree in front of a crypt. It had been placed there for a young man pictured in a baseball cap who had died when he was only nineteen.

Just how important the spiritual practice of remembering the dead is became clear to me when I spent a morning a few days before Christmas with my friend Pierino Sciubba visiting the main cemetery in his hometown of Guardiagrele. Though it was a chilly day and raining lightly, the cemetery was filled with people coming and going. Like the other visitors, Pierino stopped first at a nearby flower shop and bought four bunches of yellow and white mums to place at his family members' crypts. The cemetery supplies vases and buckets as well as water spigots so people can refresh the flowers they bring. Ladders are provided in case your loved one happens to be buried in a top crypt too high for you to reach.

Sometimes crypts display multiple photographs of the deceased. That was the case with the nineteen-year-old whose family had left a decorated Christmas tree. The photos show him at various ages, always against a backdrop of the sea. He must have loved being by water. Touching messages often appear at the gravesites, offering glimpses into the character of the person who died. As if sending a message from the world beyond, the tomb of Filomena Di Crescenzo, Pierino's mother-in-law, is engraved with the words *I will love you from the heavens as I did on earth.*

The size of a crypt also might say something about the person who died. In the Guardiagrele cemetery, one of the largest tombs belongs to a man whose family owns a marble business. It is big enough for you to walk inside it, as you would a small chapel. There are several laminated photos of the man, who appears to have died in his fifties. The gravesite seems to scream, "Look at me. I was rich, important." It reminded me of Percy Bysshe Shelley's poem *Ozymandias*: "Look on my Works, ye Mighty, and despair / Nothing beside remains." Still, I would be the last one to want to deprive anyone of their wish to be remembered in a broad, ostentatious way.

Pierino's parents and his brother-in-law are buried at the same gravesite. One day, he and his sister, his wife, his daughter, and his son-in-law will likely be buried there, too. It must be comforting to know where one's final resting place will be. I have no idea where I will be buried, or who will be my companions. My grandparents, aunts, and uncles are in two different cemeteries in New Jersey, the state where I was born. My parents are buried in Texas, where they moved after they retired. My husband wishes to be cremated. I don't. Someday, I will have to sort all this out.

Soon a white-haired man shuffles past me on his way to a nearby gravesite. In a rather amazing show of strength for someone so frail-looking, he hoists himself on top of one of the crypts. The sight makes me a little anxious: This particular crypt is on the edge of a steep hill and I fear the man might fall off or, worse, jump. He stays on his knees on top of the crypt for several moments, his head bowed. When he walks away, I take a closer look and realize what he was doing. He was trying to place a poinsettia plant on top of the tomb. The raw determination he showed in climbing on top of that crypt brings tears to my eyes.

On this particular crypt, there is a photograph of a silver-haired man in aviator glasses. He was born in 1945 during the war, and died in 1984, at the age of forty-nine. A son perhaps of the old man? A brother?

On my way out of the cemetery, I notice a young woman and an elderly gentleman at the gravesite of the nineteen-year-old pictured by the sea. The elderly man touches his fingers to his lips then places them on the face of the teenager in the photograph, imparting a kiss. He does this several times. Was the young man a grandson? A nephew? So many unspoken stories in the cemetery. So many lives unforgotten.

Another custom I find so moving is the practice of placing placards on public walls announcing a loved one's death. To rate an obituary in a large US newspaper these days, you generally have to be either famous or infamous. In Italy, every person has an equal chance to be remembered. Death notices on public walls aren't in tiny agate print, but are poster-size for easy reading, usually accompanied by a photograph of the deceased. They include the date of death and details of funeral arrangements. Just as often, friends, colleagues, and family members will post separate notices offering their condolences. Those might say something like this:

The friends of Lu Fucaracce [an organization] participate in the sorrow that has struck the Colacelli family on the death of their dear Gaetano.

Messages from family members are often quite moving for even strangers to read. Said one:

Today at 12:30 at the Civil Hospital of Pescara, the dear existence of Elvia Capuzzi spent itself.

The notice went on to say:

If there ever was a way to define the joy and goodness that you have given to us, it would be close to infinity, but what you have given us is much more. Thank you for taking all of our first steps with us and teaching us to walk and then to run, dear aunt.

It was signed, *Nicola and Filippo*.

On the last day of the year, many Italian churches hold a *ringraziamento*, or gratitude, service. It is a time for people in the community to give thanks for blessings received during the year. Babies born and baptized are celebrated, as well as couples who married, children who made their First Communion, and men and women who entered religious life. Each person who died is also remembered. What I find so moving is that every person is mentioned by name. It's a way of saying each of them mattered—whether he or she was a baker, shop owner, lawyer, doctor, artist, technician, or *tuttofare*, a handyman. Each person who dies leaves a tear in the fabric of the community.

I don't find this emphasis on remembering the dead at all maudlin. I often wish I lived closer to the cemeteries where my mother and father are buried so that I might visit their graves, kiss their tombstones (as I've seen Italians do for their loved ones), sit for a spell, and "talk" with them. From what I've witnessed in Italy, honoring those who died, visiting often their resting place, takes some of the sting out of missing the dead. I wish every church held something like Italy's annual *ringraziamento* services. Doesn't every person deserve to be remembered, and by name?

FOR REFLECTION

What are your customs or rituals for remembering family members and friends who have died?

Which of the Italian customs cited do you find meaningful?

What are some new ways you might honor the dead?

Many spots in Italy like this one overlooking the Apennines lend themselves to contemplation. *(Credit: Leila Caramanico)*

CHAPTER 6

An Ode to Slow

When I worked as a journalist for a National Public Radio station in Illinois, several of my colleagues would heat their lunch in the station's communal microwave. Chemically induced aromas emanating from the artificial flavors and preservatives in these frozen, cardboard-packaged meals would waft through the newsroom. My colleagues usually ate at their desks, seated in front of a computer screen, sometimes taking bites of food between talking on the telephone.

Today, fast corresponds with efficient. We want high-speed internet, automatic cash machines, and express checkouts at the store. Slowness connotes laziness, dullness, a lack of productivity. The rule of fast applies sadly to our US eating habits as well. In restaurants, customers expect to be waited on quickly. They assume the meal itself will be cooked swiftly and speedily served.

Then comes the rush to clear the table and bring the check. In-and-out eating prevails.

Italy is one of the few countries left in the industrialized world that hasn't succumbed to the cult of fast. Italians look upon slowness as a fundamental gift that adds to life's enjoyment. I remember once talking with the late peace activist Jim Forest who often traveled with the great Buddhist monk and teacher Thich Nhat Hanh. Jim marveled at how the monk would walk at the same leisurely pace even if he was running late for an appointment. Thich Nhat Hanh encouraged visitors to his monastery in France to chew their food twenty-five times before swallowing. His manner of walking and eating were part of his spiritual practice. Italians would have no trouble with this. They largely eschew processed fast food in favor of fresh, locally grown foods—something they refer to in a kind of shorthand as "farm to table." Eating in a leisurely manner comes second nature in a country that venerates the table as a place of quality, communion, and tradition.

One of the adjustments I had to make as an American living in Italy was the amount of time spent at meals. I grew up outside of New York City where people often stand at food wagons or outdoor kiosks, wolfing down a bagel for breakfast or munching on a hot dog for lunch. In Italy, eating a meal means sitting at a table. Mealtime easily can turn into an hours-long affair of multiple courses, whether in a restaurant or at a friend's home.

I remember the first time my Italian cousin Mario invited me to a lunch at a restaurant in the small town of San Giovanni Rotondo, famous for its shrine to Saint Padre Pio and the massive hospital that donors built there in his honor. The meal was served family-style. After filling up on appetizers of roasted eggplant and zucchini and then a course of spaghetti with meat sauce, I thought the meal was over.

It was just beginning. Out from the kitchen came a second type of pasta, and after that some grilled pork with roasted potatoes and vegetables. The roasted eggplant and zucchini were the appetizers and the two different kinds of spaghetti were part of the *primo*, the first course. The meat, potatoes, and vegetables comprised the *secondo*, the second course. All that was followed by fresh fruit, biscotti, and espresso coffee. I quickly learned to take it easy on those first couple of courses because a lot more was usually on the way.

There is more to slow eating, though, than just learning to pace yourself. The ingredients that go into a meal are something Italians take extremely seriously, as any fan of Stanley Tucci's popular CNN series *Searching for Italy* knows. Tucci travels the countryside taste-testing Italy's regional specialties, from Roman dishes made with offal to Emilio Romagna's prized mortadella and Sicily's anchovy-based sauces. Slow eating allows us to savor all the flavors in a phased succession of courses, while also enjoying the company at the table—without any time constraints.

An appreciation for local gastronomy and the conviviality of the table spurred Italian writer and activist Carlo Petrini to reject the fast-food culture emanating from the US and advocate for an international "slow food movement." Anchoring Petrini's movement is the belief that there should be collaboration between all participants in the food chain—from farmers to chefs, restaurant owners to individual consumers. What began as a lonely crusade in the 1980s has become a global phenomenon.

Cooking is one of the activities I most enjoy in Italy. It is never a chore. In fact, it becomes a meditative time, what the Benedictine monastics might refer to as "holy leisure," when the mind is free to roam and rest. Chopping vegetables, grilling meat, or slicing fruit might not look like a traditional spiritual practice, but if we view our cooking as holy leisure, it leads us to the sacred in the ordinary. As Benedictine Sister Joan Chittister writes, "The purpose of holy leisure is to bring a kind of spiritual-material balance back into lives gone askew. It's meant to give people time to live thoughtful as well as productive lives."

Cooking in this way becomes part of a broader ritual that also allows me to remember the people who play a part in bringing my food to the table. It is a ritual that begins with shopping in one of the outdoor vegetable and fruit markets. After a while, you get to know each vendor personally. If it's Tuesday, Federico will be under the stone arches near Guardiagrele's main piazza with lettuce and broccoli rabe from his farm. His produce is so fresh that a slug or two might come crawling out from within the lettuce leaves. If it's Thursday, Vincenzo swings into the neighborhood in his sputtering blue truck, its bed stacked with a colorful palette of red peppers, oranges, lemons, apples, and pears. You learn to cook with what is in season—broccoli rabe and squash in the winter, spinach and artichokes in spring, asparagus and green beans in summer.

Unlike the anonymous, big-box, one-stop stores so many of us frequent in the States, shopping in Italy revolves around relationships. You visit your local *macelleria* for meat, a *forno* for bread, an *enoteca* for wine, a *negozio di formaggi* for cheese, and a *pasticceria* for pastries. You come to know the individual shop owners, and they get to know you. There are now throughout Italy many sumptuously stocked supermarkets that offer faster, one-stop shopping. But why go to them? Slow shopping isn't just about buying things, it's about the friendships we build.

To practice the slow food culture, though, we don't need to travel to Italy, or even leave our home. There are simple practices we can adopt. We can become more mindful of our relationship to the food we eat. How far did that eggplant have to travel to get to my plate? How are the chickens raised that provided those eggs? How many additives are in that cut of beef?

If our budgets can accommodate it, we can shop at smaller stores that specialize in one thing, say, bread or meat or cheese. We can build time into our schedules to prepare meals slowly at home. It need not be anything fancy. It can be something as simple as slices of mozzarella and tomatoes topped with fresh basil and sprinkled with extra virgin olive oil, served on some crusty, toasted bread.

Italian cooks learned centuries ago that when we take a little extra time to select quality ingredients, and then carefully and lovingly assemble a meal, cooking no longer feels like a chore. Eating is no longer solely a means of survival. Both become a sacred act and part of the joy of living.

FOR REFLECTION

How would you describe your mealtime traditions? Are your meals largely eaten on the go, in front of a computer or TV screen, or seated at a table where the focus is your food and companionship with your tablemates?

What would make shopping for food and cooking a more meditative practice for you?

What are your relationships with the people who provide the food for your table?

CHAPTER 7

Slow Tourism

Part of the lure of being in a foreign country is the feeling of anonymity it affords. We can leave an old self behind and remold our identity, surrounded by people who know little or nothing about our past. Italians, however, are exceptionally curious about their fellow human beings. One isn't likely to remain anonymous for any length of time. I'm reminded of that anytime I spend a month or more in the same town.

This isn't necessarily a drawback. It makes Italy one of the best countries in which to engage in "slow tourism," a mode of traveling that includes spending an extended period of time in the same place. Call it traveling at the speed of the soul versus the "If it's Tuesday, this must be Belgium" brand of tourism.

On one of my stays in Guardiagrele, a town of about ten thousand residents in the region of Abruzzo, I got in the habit of finishing up my writing day by going to the evening Mass at one of the Catholic churches. I love everything about Italian Masses—from the septuagenarian priests to the elderly women who sit in the same pew each day and burst a cappella into song at the start and end of every service. I usually take the same route to and from church every day. One evening, as I was returning home from Mass, two women approached me on the street.

"*Chi è lei?*" Who are you? the older of the two women asked, addressing me as *lei*, the formal pronoun for *you*. "We see you walking here every day."

The intrusion might have been off-putting anywhere else. This being Italy, it wasn't. The women—a mother and daughter, it turned out—were just being friendly. Perhaps a bit nosy, too, another common Italian trait. I told them I was in the town because I had friends there.

Their next question: *Ah, chi sono?* Who are they? They suggested that perhaps they knew my friends.

The women were on their way to a nearby park to "change the air," as Italians say of spending time outside, and invited me to join them. I declined because I still needed to shop for that evening's meal, but assured them I'd join them another day.

Often, I have the sense when I'm walking in a small Italian town that someone, somewhere is watching me, perhaps from a balcony, a doorway, or a window. I don't mean they are watching in a sinister way. It reflects more of a genuine interest in and curiosity about other people, of wanting to know, as the woman who approached me that day on the street, "Who are you?" It's quite different from my experience of growing up outside of New York City. You learn to avoid eye contact with the people seated across from you in the subway. You might read a newspaper (folded in slim panels so that they don't brush up against your neighbor), keep your eyes trained on a book, or now that just about everyone has a cell phone, gaze at emails or texts. The same protocol exists for eating in New York restaurants where the tables are sometimes so close, you might inadvertently knock knees with the stranger seated next to you. It would be a rare Italian indeed who would hold off striking up a conversation with someone sitting physically that close.

A friend who has lived in Rome for many years theorizes that one of the reasons lines at banks and public offices are so often long, is that it forces people to interact. "It's all about *la chiacchiera*." It's all about chitchat, he says.

Staying in the same town for an extended period, you find yourself gravitating toward the same grocers, fruit and vegetable vendors, and clothing sellers in the outdoor markets. This, too, is part of slow tourism, or what I like to call "spiritual tourism." On one of my stays in Cassino, I became acquainted with a woman who sells fresh produce at the outdoor market. Soon Gabriela and I were on a first-name basis. I learned how many grandchildren she has and where she has relatives living abroad. I returned to her produce stand several times each week.

One Saturday, she wasn't at her usual stall, so I bought my fruits and vegetables from another vendor. When I turned down a different street, I spotted Gabriela.

"Were you looking for me?" she asked.

I assured her I was. I didn't know that the merchants sometimes occupy different spots on weekends. I felt like a traitor for buying my produce elsewhere, so I ended up buying some fruit from Gabriela that I really didn't need. In the States, I probably would have just admitted that I'd already shopped elsewhere and moved on. Somehow, I intuited that's not the Italian way. It's the relationship that matters.

When you stay for a period of time in one place, you begin to pick up on the quirks of daily living that the local residents know, but come as a surprise to tourists. On an August stay in Guardiagrele, my husband and I learned through experience to put aside a glass of water and go to the bathroom before we went to bed because the town sometimes turns off the water supply overnight in summer so reserves don't run too low. In that case, you can't get a drink of tap water in the middle of the night, flush the toilet, or wash your hands.

Shopping protocols also apply. If you want to buy a roasted chicken for supper, you'd better order it first thing in the morning from the folks at *la macelleria*, the meat shop, before they run out or else you won't be eating roast chicken that night. Same thing with fresh bread. Shelves at the *panetteria* can empty out by noon. These are the things you learn but, as my friend the Trappist monk Brother Paul Quenon would say, "You have to *be* there."

I understand the impulse of wanting to see as much of a foreign country as possible in a single trip, especially if it is your first and possibly only visit. Of course, there are many must-see places in Italy: Rome, Florence, Venice, Bologna, Siena, Assisi, Pompei, Capri, Positano, and Cinque Terre, just to name a few. For me, the "real" Italy lies in the small towns and the lesser-known regions, such as Abruzzo, Molise, Basilicata, Puglia, Sardegna. In fact, Molise has begun using the marketing motto, *Molise non existe*, "Molise doesn't exist," to advertise that visitors to the region would be enjoying an as-yet-little-explored, less crowded, less touristy, and more authentic part of the country.

Enmeshing oneself in the same neighborhood for a period of time and experiencing the fabric of daily life—by going to the same markets, getting to know local merchants, frequenting nearby cafés, and attending community events—is a far more meaningful way to be a tourist and to encounter the real Italy. In such a way, one feels a sense of belonging, even as an outsider. Who can say? You might be stopped on a street one day and asked by a friendly stranger wanting to know, "Who are you?"

FOR REFLECTION

Have you experienced a certain freedom to be who you want to be when traveling in a foreign country? How can you experience a sense of heightened awareness about yourself and your surroundings when you return home?

When you travel, is your focus on fitting in as many sights as possible or on forming new relationships and learning about another culture? What have your best and most spirit-expanding travels been like?

Who are some of the people you've encountered on trips abroad that left a lasting impression? What is it about that experience or person that stays with you?

CHAPTER 8

Hanging the Biancheria to Dry

Laundry draped over a balcony is a standard sight in any Italian town—as much a part of the local scene as friends enjoying an afternoon aperitivo in an outdoor café or young lovers kissing in a park. There is a practical reason Italians hang their laundry outside. Americans staying in an Italian apartment for any length of time might find a compact washing machine ensconced in the bathroom next to the shower. A clothes dryer? Not likely.

There is a short answer to why this is so. It isn't that dryers are horribly expensive, but electricity in Italy is. Running a dryer multiple times a week would be cost-prohibitive for many families. There is, though, a deeper reason. Whether in a *città* or

Hanging out the laundry to dry on balconies is a familiar sight
and can become a contemplative practice.

burgo—a large city or a village—clothes hanging out to dry over a balcony or on an outdoor clothes rack is more than part of the landscape. It is a time-honored tradition, as much as throwing back an espresso first thing in the morning or sipping a glass of Campari before dinner. It can also become a meaningful meditative practice.

Hanging out the laundry sparked an amusing string of comments a few years back on the travel website Tripadvisor. One man wrote that his Italian grandmother still refused to use a washing machine even after the family bought her one as a gift. Instead, she kept handwashing her *biancheria* and hanging it over the balcony until she physically couldn't do it any longer. Even Italians who live in pollution-plagued large cities will argue that their clothes still smell better if allowed to waft outside in the wind to dry.

The gentleman who wrote on Tripadvisor also had an answer for Americans who might be concerned about displaying their nighties, bras, and boxer shorts before the whole neighborhood. He said it's an incentive to take better care of one's intimate wear. "We don't care a heck if people see our underwear hanging out," the man wrote. "Everyone does that, so who cares? Maybe that's why we take care of it—no holes, no threadbare underwear here." I can't say for sure if that last comment is universally true, but it might be a goal to aim for.

The first time I spent several months in Italy during winter, I was a bit puzzled by how I was going to dry some of my sweaters and heavy slacks. The plastic drying rack my landlord provided hardly seemed up to the task. At first, I hung my wet woolens in the shower. They took days to dry. Then I noticed that clothing, towels, sheets, and pillowcases would appear on my neighbors' balconies whenever the sun was shining and the temperature rose to anywhere above 40 degrees. I soon followed my neighbors' lead. Clothes dried much quicker in the open air than inside. Even if they remained damp when I took them back in, I could always drape them over a radiator at night. In the morning, they would be good to go.

The apartment I rented that winter came with a supply of clothespins that weren't the straight wooden kind with a slit in the middle that I remembered from childhood. They were plastic snap pins in a host of pastel colors—a delight to look at. They seemed more like toys. Not having a dryer kept me attuned to the weather. I faithfully previewed the five-day forecast and planned my washing days accordingly. I also got to know my neighbors by observing their *biancheria*. The disembodied clothes were like ghosts revealing the context of their lives. Blue overalls draped over a balcony meant someone's husband was likely a municipal worker. Baby pajamas and toddler clothes signaled a young family. I enjoyed surveying the range of bath towel colors and sheet patterns I saw. As a creative exercise, I would sometimes make up stories about the lives belonging to the clothing dangling in the wind.

Italians are on to something with their open-air drying. The US Environmental Protection Agency says clothes dryers represent one of the biggest energy hogs in any household. Americans could save an average of $25 off their monthly electricity bill if they just stopped using them, according to one prominent energy conservation group. Saving that amount of energy is also good for the environment. There are other advantages to following Italy's lead on dispensing with electric dryers—reasons of the heart. I looked forward to the days I could hang my laundry in the open air. Those days propelled me outside into the sunshine and fresh air. Hanging each article of clothing left me with a sense of accomplishment. I would often recall where I bought a piece of clothing, whether it was a gift, and why I was attracted to it in the first place.

Once the last piece of clothing was hung, I spent time sitting on the balcony, looking out at the neighborhood. Those pauses turned into important contemplative moments within my day. Instead of becoming just another chore, hanging out the laundry became an excuse for practicing *il dolce far niente*, the "sweetness of doing nothing," once the work was done.

When I returned to the US from Italy, I bought a clothesline to string up in our backyard between a tree trunk and a hook outside the back door. To cart my damp clothes up the basement stairs from where the washer is and take them outside calls for a little more effort than just tossing them from the washer into the dryer sitting beside it. Still, I've come to look at my trek to the clothesline as a pilgrimage.

I wondered how the neighbors might react to my outdoor clothesline, but so far no one has objected. I admit to not yet hanging out my underwear, unlike the intrepid Italian gentleman who wrote on Tripadvisor. Perhaps that will come. The best part is enjoying a pause after I've taken down my dried clothes, smelling now of the open air. To simply pause and be still is a time-honored spiritual practice. It is not a terribly American thing to do. Thankfully, though, it is very Italian.

FOR REFLECTION

What are the household chores that have become a meditative practice for you?

Have you tried hanging clothes outside to dry? If so, what was that experience like for you?

Do you agree with the writer on Tripadvisor that we'd take better care of our clothing if we knew our neighbors could view it on our clothesline?

CHAPTER 9

The Bells That Cause Us to Pause

An app you can place on your cell phone imitates the chimes that call monks and monastic sisters to community prayer. The app rings at certain hours and signals that it's time to break from whatever we are doing, take a breather, and simply *be*.

Such an app would be superfluous in Italy. Churches are ubiquitous and just about every one of them has its own tower where *le campane*, the church bells, ring out the hours during the day. No need for wristwatches or cell phones to tell the time.

When I spent an extended stay in the city of Cassino in the Lazio region, our apartment was located around the corner from Sant'Antonio di Padova, the oldest church in the city. It is, coincidentally, the parish where my paternal grandparents,

Giovanna Mastronardi and Tommaso Valente, were married. The bells rang every hour. Twelve chimes, for instance, signaled noon. Shorter dings would follow to signal a half hour. And sometimes quick ringing would follow an hourly toll as if to say, "Are you paying attention?" In the first weeks of our stay, the bells would wake me at night. After a while, they became soothing background music. I looked forward to hearing them and missed them when I returned to the US.

Some estimates put the number of churches in Italy at a minimum of twenty thousand—with nine hundred in Rome alone. In the small town of Guardiagrele in the Abruzzo region, where I often stay, nine churches are clustered in the central part of town. After a while, I was able to recognize the distinct sound of each church's bells by their individual timbres. *Le campane* atop the main church of Santa Maria Maggiore are so powerful their sound reverberates in your chest. They easily overpower any attempts at conversation in the street below them.

If the bells of Santa Maria Maggiore are like bass singers, those of Chiesa San Nicola di Bari, just a short distance away, are baritones—not quite as deep and strong. *Le campane* of La Madonna del Carmine Church have a more feminine tone, befitting a church named for the mother of Jesus.

Most church bells in the US ring only on Sundays. They are a call to worship, announcing that the service will begin shortly. Italian bells harken back to the ancient practice of recalling monks and monastic sisters to an awareness of God. When the bells sound on monastery grounds, they are both a call to community prayer and a signal to drop whatever you are doing and turn your attention more fully to the presence of God.

In her book *The Monastic Heart*, Benedictine Sister Joan Chittister says church bells "wrench our attention back to what is really important in life: the memory of God in our midst . . . The bells jog the memory that there are actually more important, more meaningful, more demanding dimensions of life than anything ordinary we might be doing as they ring."

She adds, "No bedroom clocks, no personal watches take their place as harbingers of spiritual time."

During the worst days of the coronavirus pandemic, in 2020, Italian church bells rang out every day at noon to honor those who had died. Bells still sound in Italy to mark important life events, such as First Communions, weddings, and funerals. A mixture of copper and tin, *le campane* have been a fixture in church towers for more than a thousand years. Techniques used to forge them haven't changed much in that time. Molten bronze still is poured into clay molds that are broken apart when cooled to reveal the gleaming new metal bell. The Marinelli family of Agnone in the small south-central region of

Molise, for instance, has been forging church bells in this way for twenty-seven generations.

While forging as a craft endures, bell ringing as a line of work has all but disappeared. Most bells these days, including the ones I love in Cassino and Guardiagrele, toll automatically with the help of mechanical timers. Still the church in Italy has taken steps to prevent modern technology from encroaching too far. In 2007, the country's bishops declared church towers off-limits to companies seeking to use them for sending and receiving mobile phone signals. The towers, the bishops said, "should be reserved for communications between God and the faithful."

Some towns will go to great lengths to ensure their church bells keep ringing. In 2020, a judge in Trieste ordered all bells removed from Sant'Ulderico, a church frequented by the Italian-Slovenian community in the small, northeastern town of Dolina near the Slovenia border. The order came after some of the town's residents, confined to their homes during the pandemic lockdown, complained about the number of times the bells sounded—550 times on weekdays and as many as 1,350 times on Sundays.

Nevertheless, a good portion of the town's 4,800 inhabitants appealed the judge's decision to the European Union, arguing that the bells represented an important part of their heritage and enhanced the spiritual life of the town. Ultimately, the original judge allowed the bells to sound again—albeit with some restrictions on how often they may ring.

I know whose side I would have been on in that dispute. *Le campane* invite us to allow our souls to catch up with the rest of our day. Their sound never fails to lift me from the demands and difficulties of the current moment. The bells remind us that there is a dimension beyond what we might be experiencing. They invite us to pause, to remember that wherever we are is holy ground. They prod us to ask ourselves, are we making good use of our time?

FOR REFLECTION

What are your experiences of hearing church bells?

What is a personal practice you use—or can begin—to slow down or pause during the day and remember that wherever you are is holy ground?

How do you keep yourself aware of what Sister Joan Chittister calls dimensions of "spiritual time"?

Bread and wine, essentials at the Italian table.

CHAPTER 10

The Bread of Life

I've often marveled at the genius of Jesus in choosing two basic staples of the dinner table—bread and wine—as the means by which he asked us to remember him and assured us of his enduring presence. Both bread and wine are essential parts of Italian dining. Still, while there can be a meal without wine, it would not be a true meal in Italy without bread.

To this day, whether one is religious or not, the phrase "to break bread" carries with it a Eucharistic connotation. It echoes the story that Luke the evangelist tells in Chapter 24 of his gospel. Two of Jesus's followers encounter him after his resurrection while walking on the road to Emmaus. They do not recognize Jesus, however, until they share a meal together. They see him for who he is, Luke tells us, "in the breaking of the bread."

The peace activist Jim Forest once told me a wonderful story, related to him by an Orthodox priest friend. During his homily one Sunday, the priest mentioned that bread was his favorite food. An elderly member of the congregation came up to him afterward and said, "Every time I see bread, I think of welcoming Jesus."

Meals in Italy carry with them that special blend of sacramental hospitality. Mealtimes are often multi-hour affairs. This kind of sharing connotes more than just sitting down for the purpose of nourishing the body. The meal symbolizes a special communion between the people gathered. In a certain sense, it is a Eucharistic act. It aims to nourish the soul.

Even before receiving its Christian sacramental connotation, bread had become a prominent part of the Italian dining table. There is also an expression, *Senza il pane, tutto diventa orfano*. Without bread, everyone becomes an orphan. Bread is so integral to the Italian diet that the word for it, *pane*, is used interchangeably to mean food in general.

I remember one evening when a young friend came to visit me in my apartment in Abruzzo and stood up abruptly at about 5:30, saying she had to go. She explained that she needed to get to the market to buy bread for her parents' dinner that night. "My father won't eat a meal without a slice of bread by its side," she told me.

Anyone who lives in Italy for a length of time knows you really shouldn't wait until the end of the day to buy bread at the local *forno* (bakery) or supermarket. Loaves often sell out by noon. Bread, though, is more than a culinary experience. Its prominence is responsible for one of the most delightful experiences anyone can have wandering around an Italian town in the early morning hours. My Italian professor, Dr. Jessica Sciubba, spent ten years living in the US, then returned to the town where she was born in the Abruzzo region. She wrote to me of one of her favorite experiences after moving back home:

> There's nothing more comforting and heartwarming than walking around the narrow streets of my hometown around 8:30 a.m. Every morning, the comforting and crisp fragrance of freshly baked bread coming from one of the historic bakeries in the town's center permeates every street, every piazza, and every corner . . . Every single day of the week the sacred ritual of baking bread repeats itself through the wise, skillful work of the hardworking bakers all around town who fill our tables with their precious multi-shaped loaves. For most Italians, no meal is complete without a slice of bread to accompany it. Well, more than one piece I would say, and even better if the bread is fresh with a crisp crust and a fragrant, soft interior.

Mornings like this, infused with the enticing aroma of freshly baking bread, often fill me with gratitude, as it did my friend. And if you don't think that is also a spiritual experience, perhaps think again!

Even famous chefs wax poetic about bread's unique qualities and its eminence within Italian life. "Talking about bread to a Sicilian," says chef Ciccio Sultano of Sicily, "is like talking about fish to an angler, about grazing with a shepherd, or about silence with a monk." He adds, "Bread is everything and most of the time it is enough by itself."

Bread has reigned supreme on Italian tables since before Roman times. Studies have shown that the average Italian today eats about a half pound of bread daily. Bread bakers are considered artisans who use methods and recipes passed down from one generation to the next. There are certain yeasts known as *lievito madre,* "mother yeast," passed on for centuries from household to household, baker to baker. A long fermentation process that can take from several hours to several days, depending on the type of bread, is also what gives Italian bread its distinctive taste and texture.

While the four basic ingredients—flour, water, yeast, and salt—haven't changed for centuries, they combine to produce many different versions of Italian bread. From Veneto comes *ciabatta,* a long, flat bread used in sandwiches and for dipping. *Focaccia* from Liguria is another flat bread, usually flavored with olive oil, sometimes topped with herbs. The island of Sardinia is known for its *pane carasau,* also called *carta da musica* for its square shape and paper-thin texture, reminiscent of sheet music.

From Puglia comes *pane altamura*, made from durum wheat, whose ingredients and means of production are strictly regulated. There is mention of Puglia's *pane altamura* as far back as the writings of the ancient Roman poet Horace. One of my favorites is *pane pizza*, another crispy flatbread salted on top that I discovered in the Abruzzo region. There are other breads too numerous to name here. Suffice it to say that all are a far cry from the soft, mass-produced, sugar-loaded loaves prepackaged in plastic that pass for bread in so many US supermarket aisles.

Bread was once one of the most affordable foods in the Italian diet. Sadly, in recent years inflation has increased the price, due to rising grain costs in Italy resulting from Russia's war with Ukraine, as Italy imported a great deal of grain from Russia before the war. What once cost one to two euros (approximately $1.10 to $2.10) for a standard loaf of hard-crust white bread now costs twice as much. Still, that might be the price you pay in the States for a store-brand loaf of white or wheat bread full of air and low on taste. More hearty, healthy artisan bread might cost as much as $5 or $6 a loaf, putting high-quality bread out of range for many families. To my mind, making bread affordable to families of every income level is a moral imperative. Government would be justified in stepping in to control prices if they rose too much, as the Italian government threatened to do in a different case, when the price of pasta kept rising as the war in Ukraine went on. Consumers also threatened to wage a "pasta strike" unless prices came down. Luckily, the threat of both a consumer boycott and government regulation was enough to lower prices, at least in the short term. Shouldn't bread also be something that all families, no matter what their income level, can easily afford?

Even before the rise in prices, Italians showed great ingenuity in not wasting this important staple. In the US, about 240 million slices of bread are thrown away each year, according to the environmental research group *Earth.Org*. Indeed, bread is the most wasted food in America. By contrast, Italians have built an entire cuisine around the use of stale bread, known as *pane raffermo*. These slices are repurposed as the basis of *bruschetta*, toasted bread covered with olive oil, tomatoes and basil, sautéed mushrooms, or another topping. They might be mixed with eggs and milk to make *polpette*, a meatball-shaped food. Or, those stale pieces might be ground into bread crumbs, cut up, and placed in soups, or as added bulk to a cup of warmed milk with a splash of espresso in it.

It's no wonder then that we talk about "the bread of life" not only in the basic sense of bread as a fundamental building block of life, but also in the Christian sense, recalling Christ's presence in the Eucharist. Italians seem to understand this more profoundly than most. Jim Forest, the peace activist, told me another fascinating story about an immigrant woman he knew who worked in one of the Las Vegas casinos and was horrified at the amount of uneaten bread the casino restaurant threw out each day. "They make me throw away the body of Christ!" she lamented. The woman eventually quit her job.

One can imagine what culinary delights Italians might create with that unwanted, tossed out, but still sacred bread.

FOR REFLECTION

Have you ever thought about looking upon bread as more than a food staple, as representing something sacred and sacramental? Does that point of view make sense to you?

How wasteful are you with bread? With other foods?

Do you view it as a moral imperative that the price of healthy, good-quality bread be affordable to all, no matter what one's income level?

Pecorino cheese made in Abruzzo is one of the treasures of Italian cuisine.

CHAPTER 11

Business as Unusual

In the eight years that I reported for the *Wall Street Journal*, I covered business in both the US and Europe. On many stays in Italy since then, I've had the chance to witness up close how many Italian businesses operate. There are some dramatic differences in how Italians and Americans conduct business. In the US, becoming bigger, increasing profits, paying out fat shareholder dividends, and providing corporate officers with hefty compensation packages are key drivers. In Italy, large and small family-owned enterprises still propel the economy. History and tradition play starring roles. Still, Italian businesses manage not only to survive, but to thrive. Italy remains Europe's fourth-largest economy, behind the more populous countries of Germany, the United Kingdom, and France. You might say many Italian enterprises don't practice business as usual, but what I'd call business as *unusual*. Here are the stories of three Italian businesses. They illustrate some of the counterintuitive attitudes that characterize doing business in Italy—as well as some lessons they hold for us perhaps worth emulating.

Manufacturing Happiness

On a busy street watched over by two grand peaks of the Apennine Mountains in the rustic town of Sulmona, a stone building sits like a large, rectangular white cake, trimmed in blue icing.

To step inside is a bit like walking into Willy Wonka's chocolate factory. Carefully arranged in glass cases are colorful flower bouquets, elaborate crosses, even rosary beads. They are not what they seem. They are all made of sugar-coated almonds. The Pelino family of Sulmona has made these almond candies—known as *confetti*—for more than a hundred years.

If you've ever attended a wedding in Italy or the marriage of Italian American friends, it's likely you took home a small lace gift bag tied with a bow and filled with *confetti* wedding favors. The name derives from the candy's resemblance to the bits of white *confetti* it was traditional to shower over newly married couples for good luck. So deeply are these candied almonds embedded in Italy's culture that there is even a scene in the popular Italian-made series *The Bulletproof Heart (Una pallottola nel cuore*) in which a lead character teaches another character how to wrap *confetti* favors for a wedding.

At Confetti Pelino, a thin, lanky man with a tuft of white hair wearing corduroy trousers and a tweed jacket briskly descends a winding staircase that leads to the Pelino factory's lobby. He looks as though he could be dashing off to teach a philosophy class. He is Mario Pelino, a member of the seventh generation of the Pelino family to make *confetti*. While we chat, dozens of women in pink smocks delicately arrange "bouquets" of multi-colored *confetti* for upcoming weddings and other celebrations so that the lobby looks more like a flower shop than a candy factory.

The first thing Mario wants to show me, though, isn't the colorful candies displayed in glass cases or stacked in attractive pale-blue and white boxes along a retail counter. He takes me to a wall where his Pelino ancestors form a neat vertical row in photos, beginning with his ancestor Bernardino, who began making candy in 1783. This particular factory has been in the same spot since the late 1880s. The manufacturing process has changed—machines once operated by steam now run on electricity and have become more efficient over the decades. Still, the candies remain largely the same. In a nod to history, the family preserved and displays some of the antique machinery, like the apparatus that once removed the almonds' outer skin and shot the nuts into pans to be covered in hot, liquid sugar.

The Italian economic engine thrives on independent, family-owned businesses like Confetti Pelino. What's admirable is how families hold on to these businesses for so many generations. History and family pride combine to keep the business successful. Pride in the product serves as an extension of family honor.

There is a lesson to be learned here. When I was a *Wall Street Journal* reporter, I reported on many independent or family-owned businesses that allowed themselves to be acquired when venture capitalists or a large, multinational corporation came courting. Food companies, candy makers, gum manufacturers, mattress makers, furniture makers, shoemakers—even the company that once built Steinway pianos—were taken over, often with sorry results for the company's workers and its product. In today's fast-changing global economy, few could blame the Pelinos if they caved in to pressure to sell to a multinational candymaker or food company. Just as candy-making techniques have changed, so has the city of Sulmona. Even Mario Pelino recognizes it. Sulmona once was a hub for winemaking and pasta production. "Now everything has disappeared except us," he says.

When I ask Mario why his family hasn't yet merged with a larger company, he gives me a puzzled look. We are standing on a rooftop ledge, overlooking a garden near a portion of the factory building where the family used to reside. Neatly trimmed hedges form rectangles and squares. Tall cedar and pine trees dot the garden. I imagine Mario running between them as a boy. "I was born over there," he says, pointing to an original part of the factory. "I grew up in that garden. Why should I sell? For what? Money? This is my past. I would be selling my past."

Still, Confetti Pelino has continued to move with the times. Mario says he is proud of the fact that his company produced wedding favors for the first same-sex couple—two women—married civilly in Italy eighteen years ago. It has also updated what it calls the "soul" of its candies, meaning the nuts it uses. In addition to almonds, today's *confetti* might be made of pistachio, hazelnut, or a chocolate interior.

Mario also likes to share another interesting fact: the small role his factory and other candymakers played in slowing the slave trade. In the 1800s, candy companies like his used sugar from cane cut for the most part by slaves in British, Spanish, and Portuguese colonies. After the companies switched to beet sugar, the sugarcane industry suffered. Fewer slaves were needed for cane cutting. As Mario explains, that change accidentally, but fortuitously, helped curtail the slave trade.

Though he is now in his late sixties, Mario says he has no intention of retiring. "All the time I've loved what I was doing," he says. Pointing to the candy shop's entrance, he says, "All the people who come across that door are coming here for a happy occasion. I've never seen anyone cry in here."

It would be a shame indeed if the Pelino name disappeared from Italian commerce the way household names of many US companies have vanished (think Pan Am, Woolworth, TWA, Chrysler, Oldsmobile, Borders). Fortunately, Mario's son and nephew now help run the company, ushering in an eighth generation. Still, in a global food economy, the Pelinos risk not being able to keep their company independent indefinitely. One advantage they have is the vaunted place that family businesses hold in Italian commerce. Right now, given how integral the Pelino name is to the candies they make, it's a fairly good bet that the large white and blue factory in Sulmona will continue to hum in its current place. Happy people, as Mario says, will continue to pass through its doors. And Pelino *confetti* will grace the tables of wedding celebrations for years to come.

Where Z Doesn't Stand for *Zorro*

A lime-green house stands out amid the mainly sandstone-colored homes on a quiet residential street in the small hilltop community of Navelli, about twenty-two miles from the Confetti Pelino factory in Sulmona. An enormous black Z crosses the front of the house. If you watch reruns of old TV shows, it might remind you of the sword-slashed Z that was the famous mark of the masked crusader Zorro. The Z in Navelli represents something far different. It stands for *zafferano*—saffron—which is the agricultural gold of this part of Italy.

This part of the Abruzzo region is ground zero for growing the sought-after spice popular in cooking throughout the world. The house marked Z is the headquarters of *Coop Altopiano di Navelli*, an Italian saffron-growing cooperative. The saffron here is considered of such high quality that a single gram sells for more than $25.

It was not always that way. I hear the story of how Navelli saffron became the spice's gold standard for the world from Dina Paoletti and Valentino DiMarzio, whose families have been cultivating saffron bulbs here for generations. It is a story of both Italian ingenuity and the benefits found in fostering community, stability, cooperation, and tradition. All good spiritual values, I might add!

In the late 1960s and early 1970s, saffron producers from Iran and China were outcompeting Italian farmers on price. Buds grown in Iran and China mainly produce yellow saffron. Italian bulbs, on the other hand, produce red stems, widely considered to be more savory, but also more expensive and time-consuming to grow. When the price war broke out, some Italian farmers unable to sell their saffron fed their bulbs to animals just to cut their losses.

A grower named Silvio Salvatore Sarra convinced the farmers in Navelli that the way to stabilize prices was to form a cooperative. In a bit of marketing ingenuity, Silvio's sister Gina suggested he appear on a popular Italian television program to sing the praises of Italian saffron as opposed to the imported kind. Appealing to a sense of pride and nationalism—and because they were right about the quality of their product—Italian saffron regained a prominent place in the world of spice.

Why anyone would want to cultivate a product that depends, even to this day, on backbreaking labor to pick the bulbs and painstaking work to dry the stems can seem a bit crazy to most of us. And yet, saffron growers look upon their work not only with pride, but with passion—as though it were a calling.

"It is the tradition of all the families in the Aquila province," Dina told me.

"I have been doing this since I was little. I grew up with *zafferano*," Valentino said.

When I ask if the younger generation is interested in continuing this work, they both look at me as if I had come from outer space.

"It's a part of us and our culture," Dina said. "It's in our soul. No one would think about not continuing this tradition. It's in our DNA."

It would have to be in their DNA to want to endure the work it takes to produce even a kilo of saffron. Bulbs have to be planted, and then replanted a few months later. Plots for planting must change from year to year and be kept fallow every six or seven years. Excising bulbs from their original or "first plot" has to be done by hand. The replanting or "transplanting," as it's called, is also done largely by hand.

Saffron flowering is tricky business. Sometimes the flowers are few for the picking; other days they are plentiful and require large amounts of manpower. Harvest takes place only between the end of October and the first half of November and the stems have to be picked just after dawn, before the sun rises, or else they risk drying too quickly.

Here is where community comes in. Flowers are collected one by one by hand and placed in wicker baskets and transported to individual houses where they are put on a mat to dry in the dark. Next comes the "touching" phase, separating the stigma (which contains the saffron) from the stamen of the bell-shaped flowers.

Women do most of this work, sitting around a communal table strewn with saffron flowers. Usually, several women work at the same time, and over many hours, because this task must be completed by evening. Otherwise, the saffron might spoil. Many other steps follow, including drying the herbs on a sieve over wood embers, another delicate process that must take place on the day of harvest. It can take as many as 150,000 flowers to obtain a kilogram of the dried product. As the growers attest, "You have to pay close attention." Their repetitive work recalls that of the monks and monastic women—the *abbas* and *ammas* of the ancient Egyptian desert—who spent hours at basket weaving, meditating while they worked.

The whole process is so labor-intensive that growers depend on neighbors, family members, and friends who come to the town each year to help. You could say these workers are a contemporary reflection of the ancient Scripture passage, "The harvest is plenty, the laborers are few." Still, to make sure the harvest continues, the growers' cooperative offers younger people in the community fifty free kilograms of bulbs to get them started in business.

In the American Midwest where I live, fields disappear daily where farmers once planted corn and soybeans. Developers snap up the land to build yet another housing complex, supermarket, gas station, or pharmacy. It's a trend happening across the world from the savannahs of Africa to the Amazon rainforest and Europe's own agricultural regions.

The saffron growers of Navelli are frontline warriors who daily battle what must feel to them like incredible pressure to use their land for something far less strenuous and demanding than growing this delicate herb. I have a hunch, though, that their love of tradition, history, and community—and their passionate concern for the quality of their product—will continue to win out over the temptation to do what is easy. If only that were true everywhere.

Day of a Shepherd

One of the most familiar and beautiful passages in the New Testament is that of the "Good Shepherd," found in the gospel of John. It offers a vision of Jesus—and, by extension, of God—as a caring protector who knows his sheep and whose sheep know him. When a wolf comes prowling, the shepherd willingly will give his own life to save even a single member of the flock. Though ancient society marginalized them, shepherds play an outsized role in Scripture. The gospel of Luke places them at the birth of the Christ child. The great Israelite king, David, started out as a sheepherder. And the twenty-third Psalm—surely the best known of the 150 Psalms—opens with a description of the Lord as a shepherd who provides for our needs, who leads us "to green pastures, beside still waters."

For those of us like me who don't live anywhere near sheep-raising territory, understanding the essence of what it means to be a good shepherd is largely an intellectual exercise. It wasn't until I drove up a curving mountainside road to the small community of Anversa in south-central Italy that I understood its meaning in my heart.

My destination was *La Porta dei Parchi*, the Port of the Parks sheep-raising farm of Nunzio Marcelli, one of Italy's last remaining full-time shepherds. Nunzio is a large man with massive hands, a silver ponytail, and a gray beard that drops to his chest. Thick, dark eyebrows frame his chestnut eyes like window ledges. If his physique were that of a bear, Nunzio would be a cuddly one. In conversation, he speaks softly and sparsely.

We meet in a small rustic restaurant/lodge that he and some of his family members run on the same mountainside where his lambs and sheep graze. He pulls up chairs for us to sit beside a wood-burning fireplace where he periodically throws in logs to keep us warm. He asks his son to bring us cups of espresso, pieces of a ricotta cake, and some amaretto-flavored cookies. Even though I've eaten lunch, the mountain air and these savory desserts awaken my appetite.

Routine is not a part of the shepherd's life. "If you work in an office or a factory, you know you will work for eight hours and then go home," Nunzio tells me. "I never know what a day will bring. I might have to work for two hours or for twenty hours. You can't go out for a spritzer with your friends because you have to be here," he adds, casting a glance toward a sprawling stall where his flock of 1,650 sheep, lambs, and goats are munching on hay.

Nunzio did not have to choose this life. His parents were successful shopkeepers in Anversa and he could have continued their business. He earned a degree in economics and commerce from the Sapienza University in Rome. However, when he saw young people leaving the mountainside, turning their backs on the traditional work of farming and shepherding, he said he wanted to show that this work is still viable—and meaningful.

Shepherding in these mountains is a far more rugged proposition than raising sheep in warmer climates. Here, Nunzio explains, shepherds have to keep watch constantly over their flock. The sheep can't be left alone to roam because there are always wild pigs, bears, and wolves lurking about.

Although Nunzio employs several local residents, the work is a tough sell. "This is a line of work that doesn't attract people looking for stability, routine, or a more mundane existence. This work means being involved in the life of sheep from the birth of lambs onward," he says.

Why would a man I estimate to be in his late sixties choose such a demanding, 24/7 job?

Nunzio replies with a single word: tradition. "I want to encourage future generations to do what I do. To help future generations keep their relationship to this territory."

It is a life, he says, like no other, that carries with it closeness to nature and God's creatures. "You have the feeling of being in a living world," he says. "Everything around me is alive. I never feel estranged from the seasons."

I see better what Nunzio means when he takes me into a vast stall where hundreds of his animals are eating, baying, and milling around. As we converse, a sharp cry comes from one of the ewes. We turn toward it to see that the ewe has just given birth to a newborn lamb. While we were talking! The placenta is still clinging to the ewe's body. Her newborn tries awkwardly to stand on its own legs as its mother watches. Both mother and baby lamb get to know each other better by sniffing. The nearby sheep, meanwhile, seem completely oblivious to the miracle of birth that just took place.

When two sheep come close to the fence that keeps them in the stall, I have a chance to look into the dark wells of their eyes. I'm reminded of something a Tibetan meditation teacher I know often says about having compassion for not only our fellow human beings, but "all sentient beings." I sense that there is something deep going on behind those penetrating sheep eyes. I, with my limited human consciousness, just can't access it.

I keep thinking also of something Pope Francis said early in his pontificate: that he wants his priests to "smell of their sheep." In Italian, the word for shepherd is *pastore*, which echoes the English word for *pastor*, the one who leads a congregation. Seeing how Nunzio recognizes each sheep and how his sheep gather around him, the reference to pastors as shepherds takes on a much deeper meaning for me.

Nunzio earns a good portion of his living by making the pecorino cheese that is famous in the Abruzzo region and comes from sheep's milk. He leads me to a refrigerated room where varieties of wheel-shaped pecorino cheeses hang like oversized Christmas ornaments from ropes attached to railings. He takes one of the rounds of cheese and slices off a piece for me to taste. It is a soft, smoked, cheese, unlike any I've tasted before.

"Buono?" Good? he asks. *"Buonissimo!"* I say. More than good!

Nunzio sells meat from the animals he raises to butchers and restaurants (grilled sheep meat roasted on skewers, as well as lamb, is popular throughout Italy). Our final stop is the freezer where several of the lambs' skinned carcasses dangle from metal hooks. Their unmoving dark eyes still stare from their heads, as deep and penetrating as the eyes of the living sheep I just saw.

I ask Nunzio how he reconciles raising and loving his lambs and sheep with slaughtering some of them. He points to Christ, who he says is both the shepherd and the lamb. If he did not sacrifice some of his flock, Nunzio says he wouldn't be able to earn enough to keep the farm going and raise more lambs and sheep. "If some animals are not sacrificed, the flock cannot exist," he says. "It is similar to what Jesus did. Jesus allowed himself to be sacrificed so that all of humanity could be saved."

I suppose Nunzio has a point in a practical sense about having to slaughter his animals. He runs, after all, a business. Still, I can't stop thinking about those lambs hanging from hooks and their lifeless eyes. I'm not a big meat eater to begin with, but lamb certainly won't make an appearance on my dinner plate any time soon!

Although Nunzio's older son and a daughter help run the restaurant and guesthouse, he says his younger son shows no interest in sheep-raising. Two of his fellow shepherds have died in the past two years, losses Nunzio says left him feeling pain and loneliness. "When a shepherd passes away, it leaves an emptiness in the community," he adds. "If a custodian dies, people will cry, and then there will be someone who comes to replace that custodian. If a shepherd dies, it is not certain anyone will replace him."

Already businessmen from the wealthier regions of northern Italy are buying up grazing lands near Anversa to take advantage of tax incentives that the government offers. It's not likely their intention is to graze sheep on these pristine mountainsides, as Nunzio does, but rather to put the land to more lucrative uses, like development.

I can't help thinking of Nunzio as a kind of Don Quixote, tilting at the windmills of an increasingly mechanized and profit-centered food industry. He is perhaps among the last of a breed. And yet, what Italian merchants seem to do so well is safeguard tradition while adapting to changing times. A successful project Nunzio launched is his "Adopt a Sheep" program where, for a fee, customers can adopt a sheep and receive regular shipments of Nunzio's pecorino cheese varieties. He says this is also a way of helping others better understand why shepherding is a vocation, and why his work matters.

I left Nunzio with a deeper understanding of the words of John's gospel: "I am the good shepherd. The good shepherd lays down his life for his sheep." That is how Nunzio has lived his life for decades now. An apt prayer for this shepherd comes from lines in the Twenty-third Psalm. May "goodness and mercy follow him all the days of his life."

FOR REFLECTION

What spiritual values do you see at work in each of these three businesses?

What practices of Italian businesses do you find most instructive for American business? How can history and tradition coexist with profit and innovation in business?

Many Italian businesses are small and family-owned. Does who owns and operates a business make a difference for you?

Franco Malatesta was a boy during World War II
but the trauma of war is still vivid for him.

CHAPTER 12

Of Kindness and War

If you ever need to be convinced of the futility and utter insanity of war, just talk with someone like Franco Malatesta. Memories of World War II remain vivid in the minds of Italians who lived through that conflict. Franco was a boy growing up in the city of Cassino, about ninety miles south of Rome, when war broke out. Seeking safety from bombardment, his family fled Cassino, but then had to separate. His mother took some of his siblings with her to live with relatives in Rome. Franco and his father sought shelter with another set of relatives on farmland outside of Cassino.

Like a stone centurion, the grand Benedictine monastery of Monte Cassino watches over the city of Cassino from a mountaintop. Saint Benedict, the patron saint of Europe and founder of Western monasticism, established the monastery in the 6th century. He wrote his famous *Rule* for monastic living and lived out his final days there. Believing German soldiers were encamped in the monastery, the American military dropped fourteen hundred tons of explosives on Monte Cassino in February 1944. Eventually, much of the rest of Cassino was reduced to rubble as well. In reality, no Germans were hiding in the monastery. Destroying it proved to be a massive blunder of war. Miraculously, none of the monks were killed in the bombardment, but one civilian, who had been hiding in the nearby hills, died.

Franco says that when his father returned to Cassino for the first time after the war ended and saw his city destroyed, he dropped to his knees and wept. Franco relates this story over a lunch of fried calamari and baked *baccala* (cod fish) at one of his favorite neighborhood restaurants in Cassino. Now in his eighties, recounting this story more than seventy years after the war's end, Franco, too, begins to weep.

Every so often war fever grips the US. It has happened fairly regularly in recent years, as in 2017, when President Trump threatened to rain "fire and fury" on North Korea if that country didn't stop testing missiles. Trump also announced that the US was "locked and loaded" to retaliate against Iran if the Iranian government initiated an attack on Saudi Arabian oil facilities. He previously had promised to meet any hostile action by Iran with "obliteration." It wasn't uncommon for memes suggesting the possibility of World War III to trend on social media. Many were attempts at dark humor. For people like Franco, there is nothing funny about war. The world has seen that all too vividly once again as tens of thousands died, were displaced from their homes, and their cities reduced to rubble in Russia's war against Ukraine and Israel's war against Hamas in Gaza.

Franco tells another story I will always remember. A few days after news spread through Italy that Germany had surrendered, he went walking alone in a wooded area. Suddenly, he spotted a soldier in a German uniform passing between some trees. The soldier looked to be a teenager, not much older than Franco. He told Franco he had gotten separated from his regiment and was lost. He asked if Franco might have seen any other German soldiers along the way.

"Weren't you afraid of the German?" I asked Franco.

"Why should I be? He wasn't much older than me," Franco said. "And anyway, the war was over."

Just like that, people who might have tried to kill one another a few days earlier engaged in polite conversation at the edge of a wood. Here is the part of the story that touched me the most. In the war years, Franco carried a small tin around his neck containing a few pieces of dry bread. It was something his father insisted he keep with him as meager insurance against starvation. Franco removed the tin from around his neck and gave his bread to the

German soldier. That's when I started to cry at the restaurant table. A small gesture, but one of profound compassion.

Franco's experience echoes some powerful words Thomas Merton wrote during the Vietnam War, words that remain as resonant today as when he wrote them. In his book *No Man Is an Island*, Merton reminds us:

> Violence "rests on the assumption that the enemy and I are entirely different: the enemy is evil and I am good. The enemy must be destroyed and I saved. But love sees things differently. It sees that even the enemy suffers from the same sorrows and limitations that I do . . . Death is the same for both of us . . . War is both his enemy and mine."

That was certainly true in that moment in the woods for Franco and the German soldier.

I happened to be in Italy when Russia invaded Ukraine in February 2022. Italians reacted with fear and at times disbelief. The attack occurred in a manner all too reminiscent of Germany's 1939 invasion of Poland at the start of World War II. There was anxiety that because of NATO's support for Ukraine, the conflict could spread to other countries and escalate into a nuclear conflagration between Russia and the US. Italians naturally worried about what the economic sanctions placed on Russia and the effects of war would do to grain and fuel prices (Italy at the time obtained 40 percent of its natural gas from Russia and imported wheat from both Russia and Ukraine). Broader than the sentiment of concern was that of sorrow. Sorrow that widespread war might erupt once again within the European family of nations. It was as though a family trust had been violated.

Italy swiftly accepted more than 115,000 Ukrainian refugees and remained steadfast in its support of Ukraine's sovereignty, even as its own economic interests suffered. But unlike Franco's compassionate response to the German soldier he encountered in the woods, few incidents of this war are able to turn one's heart from despair. Russian air defenses have bombed civilian apartment buildings, train stations full of families, even a maternity hospital. Men with hands bound have been lined up and shot point-blank in the head. This kind of evil only begets more evil, suffering, and hate. After one elderly Ukrainian woman saw her fourteen-year-old grandson and his two friends torn to shreds by a Russian missile, she told a reporter, "God says you should love your enemy. It is impossible. I have only hate. I wish I could kill them myself, those who came here." And yet, "loving one's enemy" is just what Franco showed was possible in his encounter with the young German at the end of another brutal war.

I once had the opportunity to interview spirituality author and peace activist Jim Forest about the practice of nonviolence for *U.S. Catholic* magazine. Like his mentor, Catholic Worker founder Dorothy Day, Jim believed that there is no such thing as a "just war," that killing another human being in any context is contrary to all gospel values. Yet Jim was realistic enough to recognize that, human nature being what it is, conflict will always be with us. The best way to stop war is to avert it in the first place, he said.

Still, few of us have the power to prevent war once that engine starts rolling. We might not be able to avert war, but Jim says there is something we *can* do. We can engage in acts of nonviolent resistance. It begins with striving within our own lives to become what Jim called "islands of peace." When I asked him what that meant, his answer was somewhat surprising. "Learning to walk more slowly," he said. "Learning to breathe more mindfully, to take unwelcome tasks like washing the dishes and waiting in line in the supermarket and making them into sacramental events. Praying instead of grumbling." Praying instead of fighting.

To Jim Forest's list, I would add Franco's example of modeling random acts of kindness. In that case, the kindness offered was to a stranger and a former enemy. Franco's story over lunch that day reminded me that each encounter we have is an opportunity not only to practice random kindness, but also to become an "island of peace." These individual acts taken together can have a collective impact. In such a way, entire countries have a chance of becoming "islands of peace." Just ask Franco.

FOR REFLECTION

Have you had an experience that drove home for you the futility of war?

Would you have reacted as charitably as Franco did in encountering an "enemy"?

What practices in your own life can allow you to become an "island of peace"?

An Italian farmhouse converted to a B&B in San Benedetto in Perillis.
(Credit: Leila Caramanico)

CHAPTER 13

Looking for the Beauty at Hand

The novelist Fyodor Dostoevsky famously wrote that "the world will be saved by beauty." It was a favorite line of Catholic Worker founder Dorothy Day. Though Day lived much of the time in a Catholic Worker house in the bustling East Village neighborhood of Lower Manhattan, she reveled in spotting a single new bud on a tree seen from her second-floor bedroom window. She often noted such moments in her diary. Day understood that beauty connects us with the divine in whatever form or meaning we ascribe to that word.

The Benedictine writer Sister Macrina Weiderkehr writes of how important it is for every person to find "a magic spot," a place of beauty where one can go to simply *be*. Her own magic place was in a section of a grain field she had swept clean and put down a rug on. If you don't already have a magic spot, Sister Macrina wrote, try looking for one and "sweeping it clean."

I spent much of my career in two US cities where both man-made and natural beauty were easy to find, Washington, DC, and Chicago. Washington is a city of lovely pocket parks, an expanse of green mall and graceful marble monuments. Chicago boasts the shoreline of Lake Michigan as well as elegant early 20th-century stone architecture and stunning skyscrapers. Too much of the American landscape, however, includes spaghetti bowl highways, bland commercial strips, aging housing projects, dilapidated downtowns, and cookie-cutter suburbs.

In Italy, you don't have to look far. Beauty is often at every step. It might be found in the *vicoli*—the narrow streets of a 12th-century village—or a stone watchtower, an ornate iron gate, a marble arch, or a fresco-covered church. When I am in Abruzzo, I never tire of looking out on the soaring, snow-capped Apennines, or the amber, yellow, and pink pastel-colored houses that line the streets.

In Sicily, the terraced olive groves or vineyards are a continuous delight. Strolling an ordinary street, one might encounter the surprising sight of a carved statue of the Madonna, perched in the alcove of a building, or a painting covering a public wall.

Who knows what artists created the sculpture or mural or why they placed it there? I do know that if I feel fatigued by a day's writing work, these sights never fail to revive me.

I no longer live in Chicago, but in a college town amid the prairie landscape of central Illinois. The sights of the prairie, mostly flat fields, are far less dramatic. But Italy taught me to readjust my focus. Without dramatic natural or artistic beauty around me, I've learned to look more deeply for the beauty at hand. It might be a colorful pattern of fallen autumn leaves strewn across a sidewalk, or the mixture of purple coneflowers next to the yellow blossoms of black-eyed Susans rising up from a field, or the tiny Art Deco details carved into the façade of an early 20th-century building.

Many countries are quick to dispense with the old, no matter how elegant a building or historic a neighborhood might be, all in the name of "renewal." Whole neighborhoods in Chicago were razed in the 1960s to make way for a highway. In my current college town, a lovely stone church was torn down and replaced with a CVS pharmacy. So much for sacred space!

Destroying historic buildings in Italy is nearly impossible. Even elsewhere, it is sometimes possible to save a building when citizens raise a clamor, though such successes are rare. For years, a regal Art Deco building served as the headquarters of a national insurance company in the town where I live. When the company moved out, the building stood vacant for years. It was a given that the structure would be demolished. Fortunately, enough citizens protested. The building still stands, owned now by a developer who has pledged to renovate it so that its original elegance will radiate for generations to come. This, though, is more the exception than the rule. There is talk now of tearing down another building decorated with distinctive murals painted decades ago by beloved local artists. The cycle continues.

I probably would not appreciate these buildings as much if I had not spent time in Italy. That experience taught me to seek beauty in my daily surroundings and to cherish it. Beauty connects us to a place. It allows us to experience grace wherever we are, which is both a spiritual and very Italian way of looking at the world.

FOR REFLECTION

In what ways do you seek beauty in your daily surroundings?

Do you have a "magic spot" to which you can retreat?

Where have you found surprising moments of grace or instances of beauty?

CHAPTER 14

Chiaroscuro

Much of this book has so far focused on the many positive lessons we can derive from life in Italy. Any exploration would be unbalanced—indeed incomplete—if it did not also delve into those aspects of Italian life that can serve as cautionary tales for other countries. One such topic ripe for exploration are the deep tentacles of organized crime that still stretch into many parts of Italy. I begin, though, with the plotline of a classic Italian-language film from 1948.

In Vittorio De Sica's *Ladri di biciclette* (*Bicycle Thieves*), a young boy's idealized image of his father is shattered after he witnesses his parent trying to steal a bicycle. The father isn't a petty thief. His own bicycle was stolen on his first day at his new job, which involved cycling around town pasting placards on walls. Without a bicycle, the father can't do his work. He risks getting fired and losing the family's sole means of support. The film ends in ambiguity. It is far from clear whether with time and maturity the son will recognize that his father's crime was prompted by desperation, and will forgive him.

I can identify with the young boy's disillusionment when I confront some of the more uncomfortable aspects of life in my beloved Italy. Chief among them is a decades-long tolerance of Mafia meddling in business and politics. Mafia influence still stymies meaningful economic development in some of the poorest regions of the country. Political leaders, judges, activists, and ordinary citizens who dared to challenge the mob have ended up dead. At various periods, an unholy alliance took hold between the Mafia, certain conservative factions of the government, and violent extremist groups. Together, they sowed fear as a way to curb civil rights, all under the pretense of maintaining stability, law, and order. This is Italy's shadow side, a form of chiaroscuro baked into a country of otherwise considerable light. For those of us in other countries, Italy's experience offers a forewarning of what results when corruption draws its tentacles across the highest reaches of government and commerce, and fear becomes a weapon to manipulate public opinion.

Italian cinema provides one of the best entrées for gaining insight into this dark corner of Italy's past. Director Marco

Tullio Giordana's film *I centi passi* (*One Hundred Steps*) is particularly instructive. It recounts the real-life story of Giuseppe "Peppino" Impastato, a young activist who challenges the Mafia in his small Sicilian community. The mob's reach is so widespread that even Impastato's favorite uncle is a syndicate boss. Mafia dons provided Impastato's father with help opening the family's pizza business. The young activist's home is a mere one hundred steps (hence the title of the film) from where the town's chief crime boss lives.

When his uncle is killed by syndicate rivals in a car bombing, Impastato decides to fight back. He and some friends build a makeshift radio station and begin broadcasting scathing satirical reports about local Mafia figures. At first, the dons treat Impastato as little more than a pesky fly. When he revs up the criticisms and begins naming names, they move into high gear. Walking home from his pizzeria one evening, Impastato's father is hit by a car under suspicious circumstances. Impastato's grief emboldens him to run for local elective office. He never gets the chance. One night, stopped at a train crossing in a deserted part of town, he is forcibly pulled from his car, beaten, and dragged to some out-of-the-way railroad tracks, where his assailants detonate dynamite over his body.

Incredibly, local police rule the death a suicide. It takes Impastato's mother and brother two decades to get the case reopened. Finally, twenty years later, a new investigation resulted in a murder conviction for the Mafia chieftain who ordered Impastato's execution.

In a coincidence that underscored just how violent and diseased the country's politics had become, Impastato was found on the same day—May 9, 1978—that the bullet-riddled corpse of former Christian Democracy Party Prime Minister Aldo Moro was discovered in the trunk of a car on a street in the center of Rome. Moro was the target of an extreme left-wing group called the Red Brigades, which killed his bodyguards, kidnapped him, and then held him in captivity for fifty-four days before murdering him. The Italian government refused to negotiate with the kidnappers or engage in a prisoner swap for Moro, who had been working prior to the kidnapping on a power-sharing arrangement between his Christian Democracy Party and the Italian Communist Party. To this day, there remains suspicion that colleagues in Moro's own party, opposed to his efforts for a rapprochement with the Communist Party, stymied the search for him and thus bore some responsibility for Moro's ultimate execution.

Director Giordana lays bare the Italian government's likely involvement in a separate tragic and true episode in his film *Romanzo di una strage* (*Novel of a Massacre*, renamed *Piazza Fontana* for the film's English version). The 2012 film recounts the actual December 12, 1969, bombing of Milan's Banca Nazionale dell'Agricoltura (National Bank of Agriculture). The explosion followed a series of other terrorist attacks. However, the Banca Nazionale incident set a new precedent and left a particularly deep scar. In previous attacks, explosives had been detonated at night when there was less chance of human casualties. The bomb at Banca Nazionale exploded in late afternoon during a busy time for bank transactions. Seventeen people were killed and eighty-eight wounded. The incident ushered in a twenty-year period of increasingly violent attacks that Italians now refer to as *Gli anni di piombo*, the "Years of Lead."

Both Giordana's film and the book *Il segreto di Piazza Fontana* (*The Secret of Piazza Fontana*) by investigative journalist Paolo Cucchiarelli point to the possible involvement of the Italian Secret Service in the affair. The book and film maintain that, at the very least, Italian security officials knew ahead of time about a plot to bomb the bank and failed to stop it.

The Italian military was also implicated. Munitions experts subsequently determined that one of the two bombs that exploded in the bank that day—the one that caused most of the death and destruction—was made with matériel used almost exclusively by the military. When a chief investigator on the case began looking into the government's possible involvement, he ended up shot to death on a Milan street in broad daylight.

In the years following the Piazza Fontana bombing, the Mafia waged an increasingly bloody war against investigators who dared to challenge their hold on business and politics. Between 1968 and 1988, bombings, assassinations, and street warfare between rival Mafia factions took the lives of 428 people. Public violence was by no means limited to Italy in those years, but Italy's prominence in international tourism meant its turmoil captured the attention of the world stage.

In 1992, two popular anti-Mafia judges, Giovanni Falcone and Paolo Borsellino—along with members of their families and their security detail—were killed in car blasts within two months of each other. It was then that a majority of the country said *Basta!* Enough! A subsequent, decades-long crackdown has weakened the Mafia, but organized crime still exists. Indictments of regional Mafia operatives continue to receive widespread coverage in the Italian press. The good news is that mob figures are being brought to justice. However, terror and poverty are both powerful emotional drivers. Too many otherwise decent Italians either feared the Mafia or benefited from its largesse too much to willingly violate a code of silence.

For the people of Italy, reining in the Mafia and bringing violent groups to justice could not come too soon. With the January

6, 2021, attack on the US Capitol, the United States got a taste of the kind of terror and chaos that can ensue when fear reigns and lies are fueled by those seeking power at any cost. Such outcomes tear not only at the social fabric of society, but at the very soul of a nation. Italy's past struggles show just how destructive the seeding of fear and falsehoods can be. As Italy's example in *Gli anni di piombo* makes clear, when fear and corrupt practices become ingrained in public life, the result is danger and chaos for years to come.

FOR REFLECTION

What parallels do you see between the sowing of fear that existed in Italy in the 1970s and the current political climate?

Are too many Americans avoiding a moral and spiritual imperative by observing a general "code of silence" when it comes to tolerating lies, fear-mongering, injustice, and corruption?

What are the issues about which more of us need to speak up?

Ceremonies honoring the war dead, like this one sponsored by former Bersaglieri troops, are common.

CHAPTER 15

Lessons from a Dark Era

History reveres the Roman Empire for its considerable artistic, engineering, and political achievements. At the same time, few societies could outdo Rome in terms of cruelty and repression. Feeding enemies of the state to lions and nailing them to crosses qualify as some of history's most heinous acts. That kind of darkness sadly reemerged in the 20th century within the twenty years of Benito Mussolini's Fascist rule.

It remains a deeply puzzling question how a country better known for its hospitality, fine food, music, and art could have tolerated—and initially accepted—the brutality and belligerence of Fascism. What's more, Italian Fascism wasn't a political flash in the pan. Italians enabled Mussolini to govern not just for a few years, but for more than two decades. Still today, some Italians grow wistful reminiscing about the buildings, bridges, and railroad lines built during Mussolini's time in power. The aunt of a friend recalls, "Before Mussolini, girls didn't go to school, but with Mussolini, education for all children became mandatory." How does one explain or excuse this kind of nostalgia that seems to forget so much evil?

In one sense, Italy in the 1930s seemed ripe for the rise of a powerful leader. The country was still reeling from the devastation of World War I. A large swath of the population found itself destitute. A vigorous, virile, compelling orator, Mussolini seemed just the figure of a *pater familias* for which the nation was yearning. *Il duce,* as he came to be known, "The Leader," convinced Italians they could recapture something of the Roman Empire's lost imperial grandeur. Hence, his fixation with neoclassical architecture and his attempts to colonize other countries. He wooed followers by creating thousands of government jobs and massive public works projects. He gave government bonuses to families with seven or more children. The more boys, especially, the better to swell the ranks of the military apparatus he was building. Of course, the benefits of Mussolini's public largesse were offset by a need to stifle opposition. At this *Il duce* proved particularly adept. He denied jobs to so-called "naysayers." Suspected homosexuals were treated as degenerates. Those who openly opposed him were arrested, beaten, or worse.

One of Mussolini's darkest legacies remains the racial laws in effect between 1938 and 1943 that excluded Jews from public office and higher education and eventually stripped them of their assets, restricted their travel, and ultimately resulted in their confinement. These laws also prohibited intermarriage between native-born Italians and people from the Italian colonies in Africa, including Libya, Ethiopia, Eritrea, Somalia, and the Italian-held territory in Albania.

It's tempting to depict Mussolini as a protégé of Adolf Hitler. In reality, Mussolini's success in using propaganda and brutal tactics predates Hitler's Naziism. Even before the Nazi regime rose to prominence, Mussolini had perfected the skill of fomenting fear of "the other" and twisting the truth to fit a convenient narrative. In recent years, Americans have been subjected to the widely debunked accusation that the 2020 presidential election was riddled with fraud. This lie has been repeated so often, it has rooted itself as truth among millions of voters. Belief that the 2020 election was "stolen" led to the now-infamous storming of the US Capitol building by US citizens in January 2021.

In recent years, leaders seeking to advance a personal agenda have convinced a significant segment of the population that there is such a thing as "alternative facts" and that the free press is an "enemy of the people." These are phrases pulled from Mussolini's fear-driven playbook. Is it so far-fetched, then, to consider that some form of what occurred in Italy in the '30s and '40s might also happen in the US, if such practices are left unchecked? For that reason, Italy's Fascist era sounds an imperative alarm.

Once again Italian cinema offers insight into such a complicated and tragic time. Ettore Scola's 1977 film "A Special Day" (*Una giornata particolare*) provides something of a primer for understanding why so many Italians supported Fascism for so long. Scola's film begins with newsreel of Hitler's historic May 1938 visit to Rome. It was only the second time Hitler had visited Italy and this time thousands of Italians turned out to cheer him on, with Josef Goebbels and Rudolf Höss at Hitler's side. The Nazi leaders arrived at Rome's Ostiense train station, a place I have been many times in subsequent years. Every time I am there it is with the eerie feeling that I might be stepping where Hitler once walked there. The Führer received a warm welcome that day not only from Mussolini, but also Italy's King Victor Emmanuel.

In Scola's film, Sophia Loren plays Antonietta, a mother of six, careworn by her many domestic responsibilities. She has a husband who largely ignores her, and children who treat her as though she were their maid. Antonietta is an avid Mussolini supporter. She keeps a scrapbook of news clippings about *Il duce* and credits him for providing her husband with a job and teaching her children a sense of civic duty and pride. All of Rome receives the day off to greet Hitler, but Antonietta's domestic duties keep her at home. She sends her sons and daughter off to the parade wearing the uniforms of the Fascist Youth.

There is another tenant in the large apartment tower where Antonietta lives who also isn't attending Hitler's parade. Gabriele (played by the phenomenal actor Marcello Mastroianni) is Antonietta's handsome, well-spoken, well-educated neighbor. The two meet that day for the first time when Antonietta's canary flies onto Gabriele's window ledge and he rescues it. They end up spending the day together, drinking coffee and discussing books in Gabriele's apartment. Gabriele even gives Antonietta a lesson in dancing the rumba. For the first time in years, Antonietta feels both seen and heard. Gabriele eventually confides that he is not at the Hitler parade because he has lost his job as a radio announcer. The reason? He is homosexual. In a Fascist worldview, that makes him a reprobate. He knows that this is his last day of freedom. That evening, security officers will come to arrest him, and already have arrested his lover. Antonietta realizes for the first time the price that many in her country will pay to prop up the Fascist façade of prosperity and order.

True to the film's story, Italians began to turn against Mussolini when they saw many of their neighbors carted off to prison or exile, and when Mussolini's support of Hitler thrust their own sons into war. It is heartening to note, though, that fewer Jews were killed in Italy than in any other European country during the war. At risk to their own lives, ordinary Italians stepped in to help Jewish neighbors hide or escape from the country.

Sadly, the fumes of Fascism continue to float over Italy today. Far-right political parties, such as *La Lega* (the League) and *Fratelli d'Italia* (the Brothers of Italy), advocate hardline policies against immigrants and refugees, demonizing once again entire groups of people. At different times, *La Lega* and *Fratelli d'Italia* have both catapulted into the country's power structure, spurred on by a populist "Italy First" platform that scapegoats those arriving in boats on Italy's southern shores from northern Africa. How, then, does one reconcile all of this with the many positive qualities and depth of hospitality for which Italians are known?

There are no easy answers and any single answer will seem facile. Still another classic Italian film offers somewhat of a clue. "Fear is a drug," says the character of a Mafia capo in director Lina Wertmüller's *Mimì metallurgico ferito nell'onore* (Mimi the metal worker, wounded in honor), renamed *The Seduction of Mimi* when it was released in 1972 in English. Fear is what launched Mussolini's political career and complacency is what kept him in power. We are not immune to this syndrome in the US. We learned on January 6, 2021, how easily violence can erupt when those in power promote false, fear-driven narratives and repeatedly twist the truth.

Thankfully, in Italy, the rule of law that took root following the defeat of Fascism during World War II still holds. Throughout Italy, there are public placards apologizing for the country's complicity in the incarceration and death of Jews during World War II, marking the sites where Jews were taken. Those placards act as promises to never forget the tragic events that engulfed Jews and other Italian citizens during that time. Despite many wounds, Italy's democracy seems to rise again each time it is wounded. May it be so also in other countries where democracy appears threatened. While Italians model many wonderful traits, traditions, and practices, it is important to learn from their misjudgments and mistakes. The forcible repression of opposition, the scapegoating of foreigners, the unchecked scope of a single powerful leader are regrettable parts of the country's history that resulted in too many deaths and much suffering. This is the cautionary tale Italy still offers to the US—and to the rest of the world—today.

FOR REFLECTION

Much of this book has so far focused on the many positive aspects of life in Italy. How can one of the darkest periods Italy has endured—its engagement with Fascism—prove instructive for other countries?

How are a culture of lies, scapegoating of particular groups, and the spread of authoritarianism still problems today?

What should be the response of a person of faith?

CHAPTER 16

Trauma, Beauty, and Grace

In 2020, the coronavirus rampaged through Italy the way bands of Visigoths savaged ancient Rome. Its ferocious assault cut down young and old, male and female alike. Due in part to crowded city living and a large elderly population, Italy suffered the second-highest number of coronavirus cases and deaths among European countries. Even before the American government imposed a lockdown, Italy instituted severe restrictions. People could not leave their homes except for essential activities, such as purchasing groceries, seeing the doctor, or picking up medication at a pharmacy.

In a culture that thrives on conversation, where life is lived largely in piazzas and parks and around a table sharing a meal,

Cooking can become an important contemplative practice.
Being at an Italian table has a sacramental quality.

the enforced isolation felt for many Italians like a prison sentence. The government was criticized for not moving quickly enough at the start of the pandemic. Initially, few other countries were swift enough to realize the scope of the crisis, including the US. What Italians managed to do, however, is show the rest of the world how to respond to relentless crisis with beauty, courage, and grace.

When the pandemic began, I texted my eighty-three-year-old friend and former landlord in Cassino, Franco Malatesta. Franco told me he rarely left his apartment. I asked him if he needed me to send him anything.

"*Niente*," he responded. Nothing.

Every day, Franco's daughter left groceries and prepared meals outside his door, even though she couldn't enter her father's apartment under the government's social isolation directive. It isn't unusual for several generations of a family to live in the same city, sometimes in the same neighborhood or the same house. Strong family and neighborhood connections are one of the prime benefits Italian seniors enjoy. These connections proved the lifeline that helped many survive the pandemic's ravages.

In his book *Bowling Alone: The Collapse and Revival of American Community*, published at the start of this millennium, sociologist Robert Putnam describes how the US ceased to be a country of joiners. In Italy, by contrast, the social fabric still coheres. It does so through myriad support networks that include political, military, religious, workplace, civic, and historical organizations. Those associations have names that connote their mission: *Caritas* (Kindness), *Pro Loco* (For the Benefit of the Place), and *Legambiente* (League for the Environment), to name just a few.

In the midst of the pandemic, friends from Guardiagrele in the Abruzzo region sent me a photo of Capuchin friars walking through the town's empty streets holding high a gold monstrance containing the Eucharist, which for Catholics is more than a symbol. It is the presence of Jesus. Whenever the friars came to a house, they would raise the Eucharist in the sign of the cross as blessing. The Capuchins risked receiving a fine for being out during the lockdown. They apparently thought bringing Jesus into the streets to offer a blessing was worth it.

Italians also demonstrated that social distancing didn't mean one couldn't be social. In the US, demonstrators showed up at state capitols with guns, demanding the reopening of businesses and schools and the lifting of stay-at-home orders. By contrast, Italians still in isolation took to their balconies and serenaded neighbors with guitars, flutes, and clarinets. They threw open their windows and sang folk songs and arias.

Overworked health-care workers in the north of the country, where the virus hit particularly hard, played the national anthem over a loudspeaker to lift spirits in an overcrowded infection ward. In the skies over Rome, Italian Air Force planes traced the red, white, and green *tricolore* (three colors) of the Italian flag as a recording of Luciano Pavarotti singing *"Nessun dorma"* ("Let No One Sleep") from Puccini's opera *Turandot* rang out over the city.

Reacting to reports of people hoarding toilet paper and sanitizer in the US, an American friend living in Assisi wrote me, "People here aren't stockpiling. They are tranquil. They are worried, but they are responding with courage and a sense of humor. It's in a time like this that I remember what I love about Italy— it's the heart of the Italian people."

Another iconic image of that time is of Pope Francis limping in a light rain toward an outdoor altar to say Mass in a deserted Saint Peter's Square. It was a few weeks before Easter 2020 and he came out to pray for an end to the pandemic. He had already made solo pilgrimages to churches in Rome associated with miraculous cures during other historic plagues. Several times during the crisis, he had asked people of all faiths to pray in unison on certain days.

Millions from around the world watched on television and their computer screens the solitary figure of this octogenarian prelate celebrating Mass. It felt for a moment as if the whole world were one, and that perseverance, hope, and prayer just might prove stronger than the viral scourge we were experiencing.

"For weeks it has been evening," the pope said at the start of his homily. "[Now is the time] to choose what matters and what passes away. A time to separate what is necessary from what is not."

The pope was imparting a spiritual lesson that moved beyond the current crisis, a lesson for all ages. It was a reminder, too, that the land from which the pope spoke had survived wars, invasions, occupations, famine, pestilence, and plague during far more centuries than the US and several other countries had existed. If this land could endure, then perhaps so could the US. So could the rest of the world.

When history is finally written years from now about the Covid-19 pandemic, Italy will have contributed far more than its fair share of the iconic images of that extraordinary time. May the world remember and learn from the Italian people's example of dignity, perseverance, and grace.

FOR REFLECTION

In the midst of the pandemic crisis, how were you able to find moments of beauty and grace?

How strong is the social fabric in your community, especially regarding the elderly and the most vulnerable?

How does Italian life offer some helpful models?

CHAPTER 17

Building Community with February Madness

The San Remo Music Festival is a hugely popular annual contest that takes place every February in which singers introduce new songs composed by Italian songwriters. It all unfolds on television and just about every TV set in Italy—I'm told even the pope's—is tuned in to the festival. It's a shared national event in which Italians can vote by phone call or text for their favorite song and performers. You might call it "February Madness." It's a happy event. It's also one of the more entertaining ways that Italians are able to build community.

Community is one of the most fundamental spiritual values and lies at the heart of so many of the gospel narratives. Jesus didn't choose to go about his mission alone. When he started his ministry, he swiftly formed a community of disciples, awed by his miracles and inspired by his message of God's love and mercy. In particular, he sought to embrace within this community those whose voices didn't normally merit attention, those left out of polite company: lepers, foreigners, people struggling with physical or mental disabilities.

How do we go about building community today? Commentators in the US often lament the fact that despite having so many viewing choices, very few televised events bring the entire nation together. It's perhaps one of the reasons the US electorate is so divided currently and our political discourse so fractious. A good number of Americans receive their news from political silos that merely reinforce their preconceived views. Some folks even yearn for the days when only three stations carried the national news, and for just a half hour. All three stations pretty much carried the same news, without embellishing it with opinion or analysis. The only difference was the talking heads delivering the headlines on each of the three stations.

Few—if any—televised events these days seem to draw in the entire country. The Super Bowl might come close. Then again, someone like myself, who isn't particularly interested in football, has never watched a Super Bowl in its entirety. The same goes for the NCAA (National Collegiate Athletic Association) championship games. If you're not a college basketball fan, I suspect March Madness holds little interest for you. Perhaps at one time the Miss

America Pageant or the Macy's Thanksgiving Day Parade drew a majority of the viewing public, but that was long ago. The Olympic Games entice tens of thousands to their screens, but that is a global event. Today we have popular shows such as *America's Got Talent* and *Dancing with the Stars*, but they are hardly national unifiers. I, for one, have never seen either program. And being a winner in either of those contests is hardly recognized as a national honor, as it is for the winner of the San Remo Festival.

All this to say that perhaps we can take a page from Italy and stage an American-style San Remo Music Festival—one that would showcase America's many types of regional music in a friendly competition. It might be a way of shoring up something that has been eroding for a long time in the US—a sense of pride in community.

I happened to be staying in Italy one year at the time of the San Remo Festival. The festival is not only entertaining, it's more engaging than many of the regular fictional series that fill Italian TV stations. The final night of the judging, which is the highlight of the festival, begins with a military band in feathered hats like something Peter Sellers would wear in one of his comedies, playing the rousing Italian national anthem, *Fratelli d'Italia* (Brothers of Italy). The outrageous outfits many of the performers wear comprise another large part of the spectacle. Female singers seem to be in a competition to show as much cleavage as possible without provoking censorship. The eye makeup is, well, eye-popping, and that includes on the male performers as well. Think Boy George. The men's outfits compete for creative design. One male singer performed in a tuxedo jacket adorned with metal chains. Bare male chests abound. And did I mention the tattoos?

To be sure, despite all the national goodwill surrounding it, the festival sometimes wanders into minor controversies. The year I watched the event on TV, a male singer sparked a mini-maelstrom with his song *Domenica* ("Sunday"). Toward the end of the piece, he knelt bare-chested onstage and mimicked a baptism by pouring water over his head. The next day, an Italian cardinal objected, complaining that the festival had disrespected the sacrament of baptism. The reaction in the press and social media to the cardinal's reaction was also swift. Many suggested the Catholic Church might draw more adherents if it would just lighten up a little and let such things pass.

The festival eventually narrows the competitors to twenty-five, and then to a final three. The year I was able to watch the entire event, the winning song turned out to be a selection called *"Brividi"* ("Shivers") by the male duo Mahmood and Blanco, a song they performed hitting many high notes. Much was made of the fact that Blanco was only eighteen years old at the time of his win. Both winners were showered with multicolored *confetti* when their song was announced and then they received the gold *Leonino*, the little lion that is also the symbol of San Remo and the competition's version of the Oscar statuette. For days afterward, news programs continued to carry analysis on the festival. The winning song played repeatedly over the airwaves until its catchy tune lodged firmly in the brain. It was as though the entire country was loath to let the festival end.

Surely the San Remo Festival represents a goodly dose of fluff and marketing prowess. Still, can anything that brings together nearly 59 million people—the population of Italy—be all that bad? Perhaps, what we need to build community, in this moment of virulent division and unrelenting political vitriol that we are experiencing, is our own version of the San Remo Music Festival. Maybe, then, for just a few days, or even a few hours, we could stop arguing, stop looking at our fellow citizens as our opponents, or worse, our enemies. Wouldn't it be much better if instead we all went about humming the same tune?

FOR REFLECTION

Can you think of a time in your lifetime when our country seemed more united?

How do you think we can return to a greater sense of community and cohesiveness?

How might music and the other arts serve as a means for building community?

Italians celebrate the Catholic Feast of the Assumption, August 15, known as *Ferragosto*, by heading to the beach.

CHAPTER 18

The Holy Leisure of Ferragosto

Though written some sixteen hundred years ago and for people living in a monastery, *The Rule of St. Benedict* remains a relevant guide for achieving a balanced life, even within the secular world, and even in the 21st century. You might call Benedict one of the world's first organization experts. He divided the monastic day nearly equally between prayer, work, study, and rest. "Idleness is the devil's playground," he famously wrote in his *Rule*. Still, the text makes a distinction between laziness and something very different—the need for leisure. Benedict creates space for his monks to pursue their creative interests and is specific about the hours of rest they need. Over the centuries, monks and monastic sisters have expanded Benedict's plea for balance into a healthy appreciation of leisure time. Today's Benedictines would go so far as to call leisure "holy." It all stems from Benedict's essential understanding that there is a time to work, and a time to stop working.

A statistic that never fails to amaze me is the number of American workers who forgo taking their full allotment of paid vacation or leave time. More than four in ten workers, or 46 percent of workers who receive paid time off, say they dont take that time, according to a 2023 survey by the Pew Research Center. Among upper-income and college-educated workers, the rate is even worse. Within that group, more than half, 51 percent, don't take their allotted vacation. Why? Employees say they have too much work to complete, or they fear not having a job when they return to work. (The latter is more true among Black workers than among whites, researchers found). Others, who perhaps derive much of their sense of self-worth from their work, say they simply don't feel the need for time off. I too used to be someone in that category. A classic workaholic and overachiever, for too many years I preferred going into the office to going to the beach.

One would be hard-pressed to find such ambiguous feelings about vacation time among Italian workers. It is mandatory for Italians to receive a minimum of twenty paid vacation days—and that doesn't include the additional ten paid national holidays that workers can take off. By contrast, Americans receive an average of ten vacation days a year and often have to be on the job for a certain amount of time before they qualify for time off. On average, most American workers have eight paid holidays. Still, the amount of time off can vary from job to job, profession to profession. The United States is the only developed country without a single, uniform requirement for paid vacation or holidays.

Among Italians, "There is no Protestant guilt over taking a break," travel writer Ketti Wilhelm observes in her blog, *Tilted Map.* "The Italian attitude toward time off in general is purely, proudly about pleasure and the inherent value of relaxation."

More Italians now than in the past stagger their four weeks of vacation time throughout the year. Even so, a large portion still take their vacation days all together, usually in the month of August. This might seem like a recipe for economic disaster if that many workers take time off concurrently. Yet, Italy remains Europe's fourth-largest economy behind Germany, the United Kingdom, and France, and the eighth-largest economy in the world. The country still functions even if a large segment of the population is engaging in "holy leisure" at the same time.

There are benefits to having this communal time for relaxation. It's a way for the country to bond, for people to visit with family and friends who are also enjoying the same days off. And, says Wilhelm, "It does have the positive effect of making people actually go on vacation." There's a famous *New Yorker* cartoon that shows a man behind a desk talking on the telephone and looking over his datebook. "No, Thursday's out," he says. "How about never? Is never good for you?" Conceivably, one wouldn't have to have that kind of conversation in Italy, particularly in the month of August.

Within the summer vacation time, there is no day more sacrosanct than August 15, known in Italy as *Ferragosto*. It is a day when virtually the entire country spends time at the beach, or in the mountains or parks, or else in visits to a museum or traveling to see another city. This isn't like the Fourth of July, say, which is marked by picnics or backyard barbecues, and then most workers must return to their workplaces the day after the holiday is over. *Ferragosto* might be the starting point or midpoint of an Italian vacation. But it is always a day meant to relax and have fun. Travel writer Wilhelm calls it "a stress-relief valve built into the culture."

Ferragosto has a long and significant history. It was established in 18 BCE, during the reign of the emperor Octavian Augustus, the grandnephew of Julius Ceasar. The name *Ferragosto* derives from the Latin, *feriae Augusti*, which means the holidays of Augustus. The time off was meant to be a reward for agricultural workers at the midsummer point for their hard work in the fields throughout the summer season. The holiday was marked by games, feasts, and horse races—a tradition that continues today with the annual Palio horse race in the Tuscan city of Siena, which takes place each year on August 16.

Ferragosto originally fell on August 1, but in the 7th century, as the Catholic Church grew in power, the date was changed to August 15. That date coincides with the commemoration of the Virgin Mary's ascension into heaven, known as the Assumption or *L'Assunzione* in Italian.

Local churches in many cities hold religious processions and celebrate Masses in honor of the Assumption. Ironically, there might be few Italians left in their hometowns to observe these services. They're already on their way to whatever activities they've chosen for their day of camaraderie and fun.

In the 1920s, Benito Mussolini's government deepened the prominence of *Ferragosto* by offering steeply discounted train tickets to workers for one- to three-day journeys to allow families from inland regions to visit the seaside and those from the plains to visit the mountains. The practice also encouraged citizens from small towns to appreciate the country's artistic treasures in large cities such as Rome, Florence, Bologna, or Turin. Such excursions are still popular today and known as *le gite fuori porta*, out-of-town trips—literally, "trips outside the door." Because these train tickets did not include food, packed or picnic lunches became a large part of the *Ferragosto* experience. To this day certain foods are associated with the day, such as rice salad, tomatoes stuffed with rice, chicken with peppers, and a simple *bruschetta*—a toast spread with tomatoes, basil, and olive oil or a pesto sauce. In other words, foods one might bring to any summer picnic.

As happy as the *Ferragosto* experience is meant to be, I will always associate the day in my memory with a truly sad occasion. The first time I was in Italy for *Ferragosto*, I traveled with my friends from their small town of Guardiagrele in the Abruzzo region to a beach near the city of Ortona on the Adriatic coast. At one point beach employees began blowing their whistles motioning for swimmers to get out of the water. Lifeguards ran into the sea and began diving into the waves. A young father of Chinese descent was pulled out of the water along with his small son. But his two other sons, ages nine and seven, remained missing, probably swept further out by a strong undertow. For about five hours, Coast Guard boats traversed the waters looking for the boys. Divers were also called in to help with the search.

Throughout this time, none of the beachgoers were allowed into the water. What impressed me as I walked the length of the beach was that not one of them could be heard complaining to the authorities about not being able to swim. In fact, a hush came over the entire stretch of the beach. I imagined many around me were praying as I was for the boys to be found alive. Many of the bathers stood at the edge of the sand peering out at the water as if trying to spot any sign of the two brothers. I wondered if American beachgoers would have been so ready to comply with the authorities' orders to stay out of the water. Or would our famous American obsession with individual freedom have caused some fights to break out with the authorities?

Sadly, after several hours, divers did find the boys. The brothers had drowned. Marine police roped off an area and wrapped sheets of blue tarpaulin around stakes in the sand where they laid the boys' bodies and gave their parents a measure of privacy in which to grieve their sons. I will never forget the shrieks of that mother as she realized her boys were dead. Many Italians passed the area making the sign of the cross. Though this Chinese family were surely strangers to them, many of the women cried. The innate compassion of the Italian character shone through that day.

That night, I went home and began what became this poem for those two boys. They deserved to have their lives remembered. The poem is in the imagined voice of one of the brothers.

Ferragosto

We thought the water was a soft blanket we could throw over our heads
and pull down again, the sea a bed we could rise from.

It was the Feast of the Assumption when the Virgin enters paradise,
her body assumed whole, uncorrupted.

The hungry sea consumed my brother and me,
fickle in its calm demeanor. We held each other's hands,

tumbled into the water's salty mouth. At first, it was exciting,
the way our father sometimes rolled us over in his arms.

We became fish caught in the rocks' toothy jaws.
then separated into a silent blindness.

I remembered running between trees, how a soccer ball feels,
the scent of my mother's skin, the feel of my father's rough hands.

I surrendered to the wordless, undulating movement.
Soon my brother and I were floating above the beach,

women we did not know clasped hands to their mouths,
tears ran down their tanned faces,

men I did not recognize made the sign of the cross.
Our father held our mother as she bowed and moaned.

A pair of white gulls left Y-shaped prints on the sand.
Then I was alone. Then the birds grew silent.

I'm sure, like me, everyone else who was on the beach that day doesn't pass a *Ferragosto* without remembering those brothers, that family. It's a lesson, too, in how the most carefree of occasions carry within them the potential to turn threatening in the blink of an eye.

I still believe, though, in the ideal of *Ferragosto* as a time when people join together and repose becomes the main form of activity. I also wonder if it would not help heal the divisions in our country if the vast majority of our citizens were assured of a nationwide pause for relaxation and enjoyment, a pause for everyone at the same time of year. Maybe our Congress can stop bickering long enough about the federal budget, the southern border, abortion, and guns to pass a law that guarantees all workers and their families ample time to slow down, visit our mountains, oceans, and cities with historic and artistic treasures to see. Better yet, if it could be accompanied by discounted train, bus, or plane tickets. Maybe then we could learn to value leisure as much as our all-American work ethic. Maybe then we would see how leisure can be holy.

FOR REFLECTION

Do you feel that you live to work or work to live? How can you create a better balance between your work and what feeds your soul, your creativity?

Do you think it is a good idea to have a month that is recognized as a nationwide pause for relaxation and enjoying life?

Do you take advantage of your allotted vacation time? If not, why not?

CHAPTER 19

La Bella Lingua

Italian is hardly an international language in the sense that English, French, or Spanish is. Outside of Italy, it is the official language of only the Vatican state, some individual regions of Switzerland, Croatia, and Slovenia, and the tiny republic of San Marino, the fifth-smallest country in the world and one that is surrounded by Italy's territory. Yet, Italian ranks as the world's fourth most popular language for foreigners to study.

It's no surprise. For many, Italian is *la bella lingua*, the beautiful language. Hearing it spoken is like listening to music. It is why Italian operas such as *Madama Butterfly*, *La Bohème*, *Don Giovanni*, *La Traviata*, *Tosca*, and *Turandot* remain among the best-loved of all time. Just hearing the language spoken conjures up images of romantic evenings as streetlights blink on around

You never know what gem of artistry awaits around any corner,
like this painting of a family of workers.

Rome's Trevi Fountain, or of turning a face to the sun while gliding along in a gondola on a canal in Venice.

The more I study the language, the more it seems to reflect the personality of the Italian people. Verbs that connote emotions are used far more commonly in Italian than English. What one thinks, imagines, wishes, believes, surmises—or not—is important enough to have its own verb tense. This is the land of the subjunctive. While verbs in the subjunctive mood have few applications in English (one might say, "If I were you . . ." or "Would that you . . ."), using the subjunctive mood to express an emotion is an everyday, every-hour part of Italian conversation.

Father Daniel McCarthy, a friend who is a Benedictine monk and has long lived and taught in Rome, helped me to understand how both English and Italian reveal something about the character and personality of their native speakers. Spoken English, especially in the American idiom, is a much more dynamic language. The active, declarative voice reigns. An American might say, "We must build a wall," whereas an Italian might say, "I think building a wall is a good idea." The Italian, Father Dan adds, "is making a distinction between the thought of building a wall and the physical reality of building a wall."

Similarly, a phrase such as "I believe in God" is a straightforward statement that rolls easily off the tongue of an English speaker. An Italian is more likely to say, *Credo che ci sia un Dio*,

"I believe that there is a God." It is a sentence that uses the sub-junctive mood, that deals in possibilities, feelings, beliefs instead of making a declaration of what in reality exists.

While action verbs are a hallmark of English, in Italian, it is common to find objects acted upon. "I dropped the book" in English might become in Italian, *È caduto il libro*, "The book fell." The emphasis is on the book's action rather than the action of the person who dropped it. Quite a good strategy for transfer-ring responsibility!

Many Italian expressions also open a window onto the col-lective personality of the Italian people. Daily I discover new words and phrases to add to my list. For example, when someone needs a change of scenery, they say they want to *cambiare l'aria*, to "change the air," since getting out into the fresh air is such a lifeline for those who live in Italy's densely populated cities.

If you can't wait to see someone or for something to happen, you say, *Non vedo l'ora*, "I don't see the hour." That might sound counterintuitive at first, because often when we want something to happen, we count the days, acutely aware of the hours. But what the Italian expression shows us is that when we anxiously await something or someone, perhaps it is wiser not to fixate on how many hours must pass before we will see what we wish for.

Tutto a posto is another expression. It is used interchangeably with *Va bene*, which means, "It goes well." The literal translation of *Tutto a posto* is "Everything in its place." That, to me, says much more emphatically that all is indeed well.

Few languages can beat Italian when it comes to terms of endearment. Female friends often greet each other with the lovely salutation *Ciao, bella!*, "Hello, beautiful!" And while *Amore* (Love) is perhaps the most common term of endearment, I prefer two others: *Tesoro*, which means "Treasure," and *Gioia*, which means "Joy." Don't we all desire to be someone's *treasure*, someone's *joy*?

These are but a few of the expressions of the Italian language that continue to fascinate learners like me. They reflect, each in their unique way, people who prefer nuances to direct statements, who seek to reassure, who overflow with terms of endearment. I suspect it will take the rest of my life to master the subtleties of *la bella lingua*. I doubt, though, that I will ever grow tired of this task.

FOR REFLECTION

How does studying a foreign language add to our understanding of our fellow human beings?

What Italian words or expressions are you drawn to, and why?

Are direct statements always the best way of communicating with others or is it better to leave a bit of ambiguity, as Italians often do?

Elaborate crèches are on display throughout Italy at Christmastime.

CHAPTER 20

Christmas in a Small Italian Town

One of the most delightful times of year anyone can visit Italy is the Christmas season. In the US, the holiday season begins pretty much the day after Halloween. In Italy, it arrives in a much more concentrated package of time, meant to be savored like a fine Chianti.

I have been in Italy twice for Christmas. The first time was in 1999 as a tourist in Rome, anticipating the new millennium. My Italian friends encouraged me to return on another occasion and spend more time experiencing Christmas as Italian families do. My husband and I arrived one year in early December and settled in the small town of Guardiagrele, burrowed between the Apennine Mountains and the Adriatic Sea.

The season of *Natale* begins in earnest on December 8 with the Catholic holy day of the Immaculate Conception. In a kind of shorthand, Italians refer to the day as *L'Immacolata*, a time to honor and celebrate the Blessed Mother's sinless state from the time of her conception, thus her *immaculate* conception. Most families wait until *L'Immacolata* to put up a Christmas tree. Workers have the day off. My husband and I were fortunate enough to be invited to the home of our friends Giovanna Di Crescenzo and Pierino Sciubba to help with the decorating. Giovanna prepared a traditional midday meal for *L'Immacolata*, consisting of a first course of *brodo* (broth with egg noodles), a second course of polenta with red sauce, followed by stewed beef with potatoes and carrots.

The holidays in Italy are not so much an excuse to shop until you drop as they are a time for religious rituals and family traditions. Gift items from clothing to household goods adorn shop windows, but most prevalent among them are foods for the common table. When I asked a merchant for gift ideas for Giovanna and Pierino, she directed me to a table filled with *panettone, pandoro, calcionetti,* and *torrone*—breads, cookies, and sweets typically consumed in the Christmas season. The emphasis is less on things to accumulate than on gifts one can share at the table. It's an apt reminder of what Advent and Christmas are about: God with us at the common table.

The days leading up to Christmas include other important religious celebrations. The Feast of *Santa Lucia* (Saint Lucy) falls on December 13 and commemorates the saint whose eyes were gouged out when she refused to renounce her Christian faith. Lucy's name comes from the Italian word *luce*, meaning light. On this day, Italians email each other pictures of the 4th-century martyr, often accompanied by prayers asking her to intercede on their behalf for good health, a more loving heart, and sufficient light as the days grow shorter, darker.

Outdoor lights on houses are a staple of the season, but they are hardly the blazing extravaganzas common in the States. You might see a single string of bulbs draped across a balcony. One reason is that electricity is quite expensive. Another is an Italian aesthetic sense that doesn't equate excess with elegance. That said, the municipal Christmas tree in Guardiagrele's town square would rival many a larger city's holiday tree. It stands about fifty feet tall, decorated with multicolored fabrics in diamond and square shapes, hand-crocheted by local women.

During the first weeks of December, strands of white lights were hung vertically from Guardiagrele's holiday tree. Some residents in the town complained that the lights looked unattractive strung in that manner. Eventually, workmen on mechanical cranes arrived and draped a set of gold lights around the tree, this time horizontally. Folks seemed pleased.

On December 16, a community novena—nine days of special prayers—begins in the churches. The time my husband and I were there, three teenage boys from one of the local public schools led the prayers on the novena's first night. A special blessing for younger children takes place at Mass on the fourth Sunday of Advent. On Christmas Eve, *La Vigilia di Natale* as it is called, families eat a meatless meal of fish, cheese, and vegetables. It would be wrong to characterize this meal as a kind of fast in preparation for Christmas Day. It is more of a feast. The menu might include plates of stuffed mussels, salted cod with roasted peppers, fried cheese balls, linguine with clam sauce, or tagliatelle with shrimp. Forgoing meat on Christmas Eve is more of a symbolic sacrifice than a real one. This, after all, is Italy, where it is a venial sin not to eat well, with or without meat.

When I worked as a reporter for the *Washington Post*, some members of the newsroom staff always had to work on Christmas Eve and Christmas Day. As I was a young, unmarried reporter, I often ended up with the short end of that stick. In most Italian towns, all but essential work shuts down during the week between Christmas and New Year's so folks can travel to be with family and friends. The season formally ends on January 6, the Feast of the Epiphany, commemorating the arrival of the three Magi or "Wise Men" who bring gifts from the East for the infant Jesus. Because Epiphany is a national holiday, no one has to work that day either.

It allows people time to take down the tree and enjoy a final, big family meal before returning to one's work routine.

On Epiphany, children await gifts of candy and other sweets from *La Befana*, the benevolent witch who is a female version of Santa Claus. According to legend, the Magi asked *La Befana* for directions to the Christ child. She refused to help them. Soon after, she regretted her decision and set off to find the infant and bring him her own gifts, an assortment of sweets she had baked. She never located him, so each year she must fly around at Christmastime, looking through windows, leaving gifts for children in case one of them happens to be Jesus.

By the time Epiphany rolls around, most Americans already will have been back at work for a week or more. The slow-paced days between Christmas and Epiphany give Italians a chance to relax, recharge, and take another small taste of *la dolce vita* before forging into a new year. My Christmas season with Italian friends turned out to be one of the most meaningful I have experienced. I didn't once shop in a crowded mall or department store but spent my time and energy cooking and sharing meals with others or selecting assortments of cheeses, meats, and sweets for gift baskets for my friends. Each of the saints' days in December felt like a stop on a pilgrimage to Christmas Day. The nine days of special novena prayers that began on December 16 filled me with anticipation for when Christmas

Day did arrive. My Italian *Natale* turned out to be the merriest of Christmases. Its rituals, customs, and traditions are ones I now try to emulate every Christmas.

FOR REFLECTION

What are your most cherished Christmas traditions?

Are there ways in which Christmas is celebrated in Italy that you'd like to experience in your own life?

How can you focus more on the spiritual meaning of the Christmas season?

You Just Have to Laugh

One of the stories I like to tell about the kind nature of Italians involves the husband and wife who own a little grocery shop in the town of Guardiagrele, called La Bottega del Borgo, literally, the Shop of the Village. One Monday morning a heavy rainstorm knocked out power to the town center where the shop is located. Because I was expecting guests for lunch, I had preordered some *arancini*—rice balls made with mozzarella, peas, and a ragù sauce—that I was supposed to pick up that morning. As I made the five-minute walk from my apartment to the Bottega, I noticed that many of the streetlights were out and several of the little shops in the center of town were closed, likely due to the storm. I wondered if Bottega del Borgo would be open.

When I arrived at the shop, the door was open. Sitting on some chairs with a flashlight were Luigi and Giovanna Amoroso, the shop's owners. Knowing I would be coming by for my *arancini* that morning, they had come into the store despite the power outage. They said they didn't want to disappoint me. They had wrapped my *arancini* neatly in brown paper, ready for me to carry home.

Encounters with Italian bureaucracy, however, don't always flow as smoothly. A few years ago when I was in Italy at Christmastime, I wanted to send holiday cards to friends in France and the US. I bought stamps at a *tabaccheria* (tobacco shop) where Italians often go to buy stamps. The person who waited on me assured me the stamps I bought would get my cards to their destination. Just to be sure, I decided to check at the post office. Italian post offices are an experience in themselves. People go there for a variety of reasons, including cashing checks or wiring money, and the lines are usually so long you have to take a number.

When I finally got up to the counter, I explained to the postal clerk that I wanted to check whether I had the right amount of postage on my Christmas cards. She pulled out a large ledger and began running her fingers down what looked like rows upon rows of numbers. Then she motioned for me to wait, turned, and went into a room behind the counter. She disappeared for several minutes and went back to the same room a second time. When the clerk finally reemerged, she announced that my stamps were *a posto*, just fine, and my cards good to go.

The whole interaction reminded me of something a Benedictine monk I know who has lived in Italy a long time once said of the civil bureaucracy. "It's all about the show." Civil Service employees want their fellow citizens to know that their work is actually needed so they invent ways to demonstrate that they are of use. I wondered if my postal clerk's pulling out of her ledger and looking down its pages, her going back and forth to a behind-the-scenes room, and coming back several minutes later only to pronounce my stamps *a posto*, was all for show. If so, it was a good show!

When I returned to the States—three months after that day at the post office—I asked my friends if they had received my holiday cards. They had not. I later learned that my friend in France didn't get her card, either. I imagined the cards stuck in a sack that got lost in some airplane cargo hold along the way. Either that, or they never made it out of the local post office.

Around the Fourth of July, I got a call from one of my US friends. My Christmas card from Italy, mailed in December, had finally arrived. Two of my other US friends got their cards in July as well, as did my friend in France. We just had to laugh.

I don't know if the moral of the story is to mail your Christmas cards from Italy in June if you want them to arrive by December. Perhaps it's best to email your holiday greetings and not use the Italian post at all. This year, some friends of mine from Abruzzo told me on Facebook that they wrote me at Christmas. Their card did finally arrive—in March. At least it wasn't July.

You just have to laugh.

It isn't only the post office. I've found that dealing with any government office usually takes a good measure of patience—and humor—and offers sometimes needed lessons in the contemplative practice of humility. I once drove an hour to visit the City Hall in the town of Crecchio where my aunt Yolanda Costanza was born. I wanted to surprise her sons—my cousins—with a copy of her birth certificate if I could track it down. When I got to Crecchio, a rather officious clerk told me I should have emailed City Hall on its website, asking for a birth certificate search, rather than come in personally. Still, she invited me to write down the information I was seeking on my aunt, which I did. When I got back to my apartment, I also emailed my request on the city's website, as the clerk originally had directed. Several times afterward, some Italian friends of mine called the City Hall to check on my request. Each time, they were told my request was in process. That was more than a year ago. I'm still waiting.

You just have to laugh.

Encounters with Italian workmen are also an exercise in patience and perseverance, if not humility. Once when my husband and I were staying in an apartment that had no Wi-Fi, our landlords were kind enough to pay for a technician to install an internet box so we didn't have to walk to the local library for Wi-Fi every time we needed to check or send email. The technician was supposed to arrive at 10:30 in the morning. The landlord and his wife and two of our friends came to our apartment that morning in case my husband and I needed help translating anything for the technician. When the workman hadn't shown up by 12:30, all four decided it was a safe bet to leave for lunch.

My friends returned about an hour later. The technician who was supposed to arrive at 10:30 in the morning finally did arrive, at 2:30 in the afternoon. He was there for about five seconds before he told our landlords they hadn't purchased the right kind of internet router for him to install. This led to a round of loud talking, verging on argument, and a fair amount of hand-waving by our Italian landlord, his wife, our friends, and the technician. All this in between several calls back and forth on a cell phone between the technician and his home office.

After about an hour, the drama appeared to subside. Eventually, four green lights blinked on the internet router box, and after a short waiting period, we were able to send emails from our apartment. The router box actually worked just fine, despite our technician's earlier protestations. On the positive side, we got to spend time with our friends before the technician arrived and, because of his lateness, we got to know our landlord better, too. When all was over, my husband and I just had to laugh.

Learning some of the codes of behavior in Italy has also generated a few laughs. These practices are well worth learning if you don't want to embarrass yourself in front of Italians. One is to never, *ever*, order a cappuccino in the afternoon. I did so once and got puzzled looks from both the barista and the Italian friend I was with, though both were polite enough not to say anything in the moment. No one could tell me why ordering a cappuccino in the afternoon is such a no-no. Italians drink espresso all day! In the US, a cappuccino can be a welcome afternoon pick-me-up. Just ask anyone who works at a Starbucks. I suppose, though, it is not such a silly social protocol. I once embarrassed myself in a restaurant in Ireland by ordering a cup of tea *with* my meal and not at the end of it. I also won't make that mistake again if I ever go back to Ireland.

There are other table-related codes. Here in the US, we tend to splash parmesan cheese on any pasta dish. Just don't try doing that in Italy on pasta with seafood. Italians *never* put parmesan on pasta with seafood. My husband and I learned this from dear friends in Abruzzo after we dribbled copious amounts on our *tagliatelle con gamberetto*, pasta with shrimp, at a meatless Christmas Eve meal.

Other customs one learns along the way are quite endearing, though. I appreciate the tradition of asking *Permesso?* (Am I permitted?) or *Posso?* (May I?) before walking into someone's home. It's the verbal equivalent of taking off one's shoes to enter a home that one finds in other cultures.

I've also learned that it's futile to squabble over the bill with an Italian who has invited you out for a meal or a coffee. I learned that lesson early on as a student in Siena when the woman who was my landlord invited me out for lunch. When I went to pick up *il conto*—the tab—she told me sternly, *Non insultarmi!* Don't insult me! I admit I've used that line with both Italian friends and friends here in the US who want to arm wrestle with me over a dinner tab. It always works.

Every time I return to Italy, there seems to be yet another common custom to learn—for instance, what items you have to *prenotare* (preorder) from food shops and what foods are available on a particular day of the week. Those of us who are *stranieri*—foreigners—will likely never grasp all of Italy's dos and don'ts. Still, I always feel a sense of accomplishment when I can behave a bit more like a native. And when I encounter the less-than-efficient bureaucracy, or violate a social custom in public, it's best to remember: You just have to laugh. Laughter, too, is a good contemplative practice—and quite effective as well for developing humility. And just one of the many ways Italy has helped this hard-driving American cultivate a contemplative heart.

FOR REFLECTION

How do you react when confronted with an annoying bureaucratic delay or snafu?

How can you avoid getting angry and frustrated?

Are there other, contemplative ways to deal with these annoyances besides just having a good laugh?

GLOSSARY OF ITALIAN WORDS & PHRASES

A capella. Sung without instrumental accompaniment.

A posto. In order, in place.

All'Italiana and *alla maniera italiana.* The Italian way or, literally, in the Italian manner.

Amore. Love, as a term of endearment.

Arancini. Rice mixed with egg and cheese, rolled into a ball, topped with bread crumbs, and usually fried.

Baccala. Cod fish.

Banca Nazionale dell'Agricoltura. National Bank of Agriculture.

Basta! Enough!

Biancheria. Laundry.

Brividi. Shivers. Title of the song that won the 2022 San Remo Music Festival competition for best original song.

Bruschetta. Toasted bread often topped with tomato, olive oil, or basil or some other topping such as *pesto* (a mixture of pine nuts, basil, garlic, and olive oil).

Buon viaggo! Have a good trip!

Buonissimo. Very good.

Buono. Good.

Burgo. Village.

Caffé macchiato. An espresso with a bit of milk.

Calcionetti. Fried cookie, shaped like a ravioli and filled with chocolate or another filling such as honey and nuts, made primarily at Christmastime and originating in Abruzzo.

Cambiare l'aria. To get a change of scenery. Literally, to change the air.

Caritas. The Latin word for charity. Name of an Italian charitable association.

Chi é lei? Who are you?

Chi sono? Who are they?

Chiacchiera. Chitchat, small talk.

Chiaroscuro. Light and dark, also a technique visual artists use to depict light and shadow in paintings.

Chiesa San Nicola di Bari. Church of Saint Nicholas of Bari.

Ciabatta. Long, flat bread often used for sandwiches.

Ciao, bella. Hello, beautiful. A common greeting for a woman.

Città. City.

Confetti. Sugar-coated almond candies.

Credo che ci sia un Dio. I believe that there is a God.

Domenica. Sunday. Title of a song that sparked controversy at the 2022 San Remo Music Festival.

E' caduto il libro. The book fell.

Enoteca. Wine shop.

Espresso. Strong Italian coffee.

Fare bella figura. To make a good impression. Literally, to make a beautiful figure.

Feriae Augusti. The holidays of Augustus Ceasar. Original Latin name for August 1 holiday, set by Emperor Augustus, giving Italian agricultural workers a summer's day off.

Ferragosto. From *Feria Agosto*, August holiday. Holiday that falls on August 15, the Catholic commemoration of the Assumption of the Virgin Mary into heaven.

Focaccia. Flat bread flavored with olive oil, sometimes topped with herbs.

Forno. Bakery, literally, oven.

Fratelli d'Italia. Brothers of Italy. Right-leaning political party and Italy's largest after the 2022 general election.

Gioia. Joy. Also a term of endearment.

Gli anni di piombo. The years of lead. Refers to a particularly violent period in the 1970s that included many violent acts by the Italian Mafia.

I centi passi. One hundred steps. Name of a 2000 film.

Il bel paese dove il "Si" suona. The beautiful country where the "Yes" resounds.

Il cibo e l'amore. Food and love.

Il conto. The check.

Il dolce far niente. The sweetness of doing nothing.

Il duce. The Leader. Moniker given to Benito Mussolini.

Il segreto di Piazza Fontana. The Secret of Fontana Plaza. Title of a 2009 book by Paolo Cucchiarelli.

Il tricolore. The tricolore, a common name for the green, white, and red stripes of the Italian flag.

La Befana. A kindly witch, similar to a Santa Claus or Saint Nicholas, a legendary figure who brings treats to children on the Feast of the Epiphany, January 6.

La bella lingua. The beautiful language. A common description for spoken Italian.

La dolce vita. The sweet life.

La Lega. The League, a right-leaning, populist political party.

La Madonna del Carmine. Our Lady of Mount Carmel.

La madre, il padre, la sorella, il fratello. Mother, father, sister, brother.

La Vigilia di Natale. Christmas Eve.

Ladri di biciclette. Bicycle thieves. Name of a 1948 film.

L'Assunzione di Maria. The Assumption of Mary. Catholic holy day that falls on August 15.

Le campane. Church bells.

Le gite fuori porta. Out-of-town trips. Literally, trips outside the door.

Legambiente. Environmental league. An Italian environmental group.

Leonino. Little lion. Name of the award given to the winning performer at the annual San Remo Music Festival.

L'Immacolata. The Catholic holy day honoring the Immaculate Conception of Mary that falls each year on December 8.

Linguini alle vongole. Pasta with clam sauce.

Macelleria. Butcher, meat shop.

Meno, ma meglio. Less, but better.

Mimi metallurgico ferito dell'onore. Mimi the metalworker wounded in honor. Name of a 1972 film, renamed in English *The Seduction of Mimi.*

Molise non existe. Molise doesn't exist. Slogan for Molise (a region in southeast Italy).

Natale. Christmas.

Negozio di formaggi. Cheese shop.

Nessun dorma. Let no one sleep, title of a famous aria from Giacomo Puccini's opera Turandot.

Niente. Nothing.

Non insultarmi! Don't insult me!

Non vedo l'ora. I can't wait. Literally, I don't see the hour.

Nonno, nonna, papà, mamma. Grandfather, grandmother, Papa or Daddy, Mom.

Pandoro. A vanilla-infused, star-shaped sweet bread topped with powdered sugar.

Pane altamura. Bread made from durum wheat common in Puglia.

Pane carasau and carta da musica. Square-shaped, thin-textured bread common in Sardinia.

Pane raffermo. Stale or hardened bread.

Panetteria. Bakery for bread.

Panettone. A sweet bread with dried fruit or chocolate served mainly at Christmastime.

Pasticceria. Pastry shop.

Pastore. Shepherd, sheep-herder.

Pater familias. Latin for father of the family or father figure.

Permesso? May I? Literally, is it permitted? Usually asked before entering an Italian home.

Piazza. Town square.

Poco, ma buono. Little, but good.

Polpette. Ball-shaped food.

Posso? May I?

Pranzo. Lunch.

Prenotare. Preorder, reserve.

Prima colazione. Breakfast.

Pro Loco. For the benefit of the place. An Italian grassroots organization.

Ringraziamento. Thanksgiving, gratitude.

Romanzo di una strage. Story of a massacre. Name of a 2012 film.

Santa Lucia. Saint Lucy, a 4th-century martyr, whose eyes were gouged out, according to legend, because of her embrace of

Christianity. The Catholic Church celebrates her martyrdom each December 13.

Senza il pane, tutto diventa orfano. Without bread, everyone becomes an orphan.

Stranieri. Foreigners, outsiders, strangers.

Tabaccheria. Tobacco shop. A place that also sells sundries, stamps, postcards, and other items.

Tagliatelle. Long, flat, ribbon-shaped pasta noodle.

Tesoro. Treasure. Another common term of endearment.

Torrone. A nougat and nut candy associated with Christmas.

Trafilata al bronzo. Process of making pasta by which the noodle is drawn through a bronze die to obtain a rugged surface.

Tutto a posto. All is well. Literally, everything in its place.

Tuttofare. Handyman.

Una giornata particolare. A Special Day. Title of a 1977 film.

Vicoli. Narrow streets.

Zafferano. Saffron.

Recommended Reading

See You in the Piazza: New Places to Discover in Italy. Frances Mayes. Crown. New York. 2019.

Italian Neighbors. Tim Parks. Grove/Atlantic. New York. 1992.

An Italian Education: The Further Adventures of an Expatriate in Verona. Tim Parks. Grove/Atlantic. New York. 1995.

Il Bel Centro: A Year in the Beautiful Center. Michelle Damiani. Rialto Press. Charlottesville, VA. 2015.

The Italians. John Hooper. Penguin. New York. 2015.

Mother Tongue: An American Life in Italy. Wallis Wilde-Menozzi. North Point Press. New York. 1997.

The Neapolitan Novels. Elena Ferrante. Europa Editions. New York. 2018.

Murder in Matera: A True Story of Passion, Family and Forgiveness in Southern Italy. Helene Stapinski. HarperCollins. New York. 2017.

La Bella Figura: A Field Guide to the Italian Mind. Beppe Severgnini. Broadway Books. New York. 2007.

The Italians. Luigi Barzini. Touchstone. New York. 1964.

Eating My Way through Italy: Heading Off the Main Roads to Discover the Hidden Treasures of the Italian Table. Elizabeth Minchilli. St. Martin's Press. New York. 2018.

Delizia! The Epic History of the Italians and Their Food. John Dickie. Free Press. New York. 2008.

About the Author

Judith Valente has won numerous awards for her work as a former correspondent for national PBS TV, two NPR stations, and the *Wall Street Journal* and as the author of several spirituality titles. Her most recent books include *How to Live*; *The Art of Pausing*; and *How to Be*. She has published two poetry collections and is a sought-after retreat guide who leads the annual "Benedictine Footprints" retreat/pilgrimage to lesser-known parts of Italy. She is also president of the International Thomas Merton Society. Visit her online at *judithvalente.com*.

TO OUR READERS

HAMPTON ROADS PUBLISHING, an imprint of Red Wheel/Weiser, publishes inspirational books from a variety of spiritual traditions and philosophical perspectives for "the evolving human spirit."

Our readers are our most important resource, and we appreciate your input, suggestions, and ideas about what you would like to see published.

Visit our website at *www.redwheelweiser.com*, where you can learn about our upcoming books and also find links to sign up for our newsletter and exclusive offers.

You can also contact us at *info@rwwbooks.com* or at

Red Wheel/Weiser, LLC
65 Parker Street, Suite 7
Newburyport, MA 01950